VicePresidents.com presents

SECOND STRING

Trivia, Facts And Lists
About The
Vice Presidency And Its Vice Presidents

DAN COEN

GLENN RABNEY, Senior Editor

FIRST IN A SERIES

VicePresidents.com presents

SECOND STRING

Trivia, Facts And Lists
About The
Vice Presidency And Its Vice Presidents

DAN COEN

Glenn Rabney, Senior Editor

Includes 47 custom designed portraits
of the Vice Presidents and 23 unique cartoons.

About
VicePresidents.com

VicePresidents.com is the world's leading on-line magazine dedicated to America's Vice Presidency and its Vice Presidents. It is intended to be an entertaining as well as educational resource. VicePresidents.com is a non-partisan site, and is not affiliated with any political party or government operation.

For more information about **VicePresidents.com**, events and sponsorships, call 888-835-5326 or email VicePresidents1@yahoo.com.

SECOND STRING
Trivia, Facts And Lists About The
Vice Presidency And Its Vice Presidents

©Copyright 2004 by Dan Coen, VicePresidents.com and DCD Publishing
First Printing

ISBN: 0-9660436-4-2

DCD Publishing Books may be purchased for educational, business or sales
promotion purposes, and are available at a special discount when ordered in
bulk. Please contact: Marketing Department, DCD Publishing, P.O. Box 571533,
Tarzana, CA 91357. 888-835-5326. VicePresidents1@yahoo.com.
www.VicePresidents.com

Design by Foglia Publications: 408-970-9562.

Glenn Rabney, Senior Editor.

PCN-2002090007

To Fans Of The Vice Presidency
And Its Vice Presidents

Acknowledgements

To the senior editor of this book, Glenn Rabney, without whom this book would not exist. It's been said that books are not written, rather they are edited. My early concept looks nothing like the final product and I have Glenn to thank for making that happen. He not only shepherded this book, but also designed the cartoons, portraits and collection edition poster about Vice Presidents, and oversaw their creation. That folks is a real talent.

To the team of designers and creative professionals — Dorothy and Arleen at Foglia Publications in Santa Clara, California, who clearly know how to create first class books. To Jorge Pacheco, a gifted cartoonist, illustrator and craftsman, whose hand created all of the portraits and cartoons in this book as well as the collection edition Vice Presidential poster.

To my family for keeping me motivated — thank you!

Table Of Contents

SECOND STRING

Trivia, Facts And Lists
About The
Vice Presidency And Its Vice Presidents

DAN COEN

Glenn Rabney, Senior Editor

Introduction

*Martin Van Buren and Lyndon Johnson share a moment
as the shortest and tallest Vice Presidents.*

Who would have thought that America's Vice Presidents could be so FUN? Who could have believed that the Vice Presidency, with fascinating stories of characters and events spread across several centuries, would supply engrossing study for people of all ages?

For over 200 years, the office of Vice President of the United States and the men who have served in that capacity has remained an enigma. A position filled with enormous potential yet often cast aside, given out as a consolation prize that was occasionally redeemed for greatness. Since John Adams assumed the office in 1789, eight days before George Washington became this nation's first president, the vice presidency has been in search of an identity, often above and beyond what the office holder or president wanted or even could envision. It has been held my men whose greatness was diminished by the restrictions of the office, by those who were able to rise to greatness despite the office, and by men who the office has turned into curiosities of history.

So why, then, has **VicePresidents.com**, the only web-magazine in the world to study the American Vice Presidency and its Vice Presidents, received so much interest? From hobbyist to scholars, from grammar school students to PhD candidates, the questions flow in. People want to know. What does the vice president do? Who was vice president during important periods of history? What trivia question, what list, what fact or figure sheds light on the Vice Presidency and its vice presidents? People want to know about the Vice Presidents. The history weaves deep.

The vice presidency, both the office and officeholder, has been one of the least studied aspects of the American political system, and therefore the least understood. From its very inception, the position was relegated to a marginal stature, as many of the original framers of the Constitution believed it to be irrelevant. The Constitutional Convention itself spent less than a day debating and approving the office. They could barely be bothered with defining what George Clinton called "an unnecessary position." In the end, their only mandate was that the Vice President serve as President of the Senate, breaking ties, and that in the event that the President was unable to complete his term in office, the Vice President would fill in for him, in a manner that they failed to specify. While the Founders recognized that a vice presidency needed to exist to insure a continuation of leadership, they did not vest the office with any other Constitutional duties or powers beyond the Senate and succession. This second highest office was virtually incomplete from the beginning, and it would have to find its own way, along with the rest of the country.

At the beginning the Vice President was considered little more than a clerk with a hefty title, and in fact was often discouraged from participation in the new government. The Vice President was not provided with office space or staff, did not contribute in Cabinet meetings, or enjoy regular conversations with the President. In fact, most often, the Vice President, upon taking the Oath of Office, would return to his own private affairs. Over time the office has grown, but even in today's political climate, just what the Vice President is supposed to do, is left mostly to the discretion of the President he serves.

To fully understand the Vice Presidency, it is best to divide the study into "yesterday's Vice Presidents," those who served during the first 150 years, and "today's Vice Presidents," who over the last half century, have dramatically changed what is expected from the Vice President.

Today's Vice President has very little relationship to those of yesteryear. Due to the change in scope of domestic and international politics, today's Vice President has the potential to play an enormous role in managing the country. The Vice President is often asked to partner with the President, not only attending critical meetings, but also providing personal insight and crucial debate for the President.

With the advancement of media and technology and the greater number of domestic and foreign challenges facing an administration, today's Presidents call on their Vice President as a positive and irreplaceable aide in governing the country. Vice Presidents such as Walter Mondale, Al Gore and Dick Cheney have redefined the office and catapulted it to a stature that will never be minimized again. Vice Presidential nominees such as Lloyd Bentsen, Jack Kemp and Joe Lieberman have ensured a quality growth in the office.

The past on the other hand was quite another story. Though one might have thought differently, it took 140 years, from Martin Van Buren in 1848 to George Herbert Walker Bush in 1988, for a sitting vice president to directly win election to the presidency. Where today the office is seen as a stepping-stone to eventual party nomination for the Presidency, in the past vice presidents rarely became President on their own. Yesterday's Vice Presidents most often served a single term and then moved on to retirement. From 1817 through 1921, only Daniel Tompkins and Thomas Marshall served two complete terms in office. From 1833 to 1916, not only was no vice president elected to a second term, but only Richard Johnson and James Sherman ran for reelection, and by the time the 1912 votes were counted, Sherman had already passed away. Over the course of 53 national elections, and 46 Vice Presidents, only 15 attempted to secure a second term. The rest drifted away, passed away, or became President.

Why the change in the stature over the last half century? While there are a myriad of political reasons such as the growth responsibilities of the President, and the need for someone of stature to be the eyes, ears and representation of the President around the world, perhaps there has been no more significant player in this change than the American media. Today's culture of expansive and sometimes invasive media coverage practically mandates that the second most powerful office function like the second most powerful office. Television, print, the Internet's discerning eye requires the Vice President to be more active. America's desire to put its elected officials upon a pedestal almost dictates a more visible and active Vice Presidency.

The vice presidency is now part of the media barrage, with the President using the Vice President to convey messages to the media, to public officials both domestic and foreign, and most importantly, to the public itself. In addition, the advent of 24-hour news needs more than one person, the President, to report. *The Vice President, much like the network news anchor and the public celebrity, has advanced in the age of media.* Consider that from 1788 until 1976, the Vice Presidential nominees never debated, not even once. Since Walter Mondale and Bob Dole first debated in 1976, Vice Presidential debates have been part of every election with the exception of 1980. The Vice President is no longer a second thought but an integral aspect of the Presidential campaign. The Vice President must present the public with an image of expertise, knowledge and confidence.

The Vice Presidency and its Vice Presidents are a study of people and events that shed a story about America and its characters. Like the Presidency, the Vice Presidency has followed the country from development, through its growing pains, right into today's age. And, best of all, the Vice

Presidency is FUN. The people and the events surrounding Vice Presidents has transpired to make the second most powerful office in today's world a fascinating study. ***Second String: Trivia, Facts And Lists About The Vice Presidency And Its Vice Presidents,*** is the first in a series about the Vice Presidency. Enjoy the facts-lists-and trivia. You will see that each page leads to new questions. It keeps getting better and better. Here's a taste. From 1789 through 2003, the vice presidency has been vacant for a total of 37 years and 290 days, over the course of 18 administrations. Where did the Vice Presidents go? Why weren't they replaced? How did this country function without a Vice President? And, why didn't anybody care?

You can't beat that.

Dan Coen
Publisher and Managing Director
VicePresidents.com

P.S. — Do you have a trivia question, a list or a fact you want to share? Do you have a comment you would like to contribute? Go to **www.VicePresidents.com**. Or, email **VicePresidents1@yahoo.com**.

P.P.S. — With so many questions, lists, facts and trivia, we undoubtedly missed a date, made some errors, or misspelled a name somewhere. If so, we apologize for any errors and will correct at our next printing.

The Vice Presidents And The Presidents Each Served

JOHN ADAMS

1789~1797

1

THOMAS JEFFERSON

1797~1801

2

11. John Adams	1789-1797	Served President George Washington
12. Thomas Jefferson	1797-1801	Served President John Adams
13. Aaron Burr	1801-1805	Served President Thomas Jefferson
14. George Clinton	1805-1809	Served President Thomas Jefferson
	1809-1812	Served President James Madison
15. Elbridge Gerry	1813-1814	Served President James Madison
16. Daniel D. Tompkins	1817-1825	Served President James Monroe
17. John C. Calhoun	1825-1829	Served President John Quincy Adams
	1829-1832	Served President Andrew Jackson
18. Martin Van Buren	1833-1837	Served President Andrew Jackson
19. Richard M. Johnson	1837-1841	Served President Martin Van Buren
10. John Tyler	1841	Served President William Henry Harrison
11. George Mifflin Dallas	1845-1849	Served President James K. Polk
12. Millard Fillmore	1849-1850	Served President Zachary Taylor
13. William Rufus King	1853	Served President Franklin Pierce
14. John C. Breckinridge	1857-1861	Served President James Buchanan
15. Hannibal Hamlin	1861-1865	Served President Abraham Lincoln
16. Andrew Johnson	1865	Served President Abraham Lincoln
17. Schuyler Colfax	1869-1873	Served President Ulysses S. Grant
18. Henry Wilson	1873-1875	Served President Ulysses S. Grant
19. William Wheeler	1877-1881	Served President Rutherford B. Hayes
20. Chester Alan Arthur	1881	Served President James Garfield
21. Thomas Hendricks	1885	Served President Grover Cleveland
22. Levi Parsons Morton	1889-1893	Served President Benjamin Harrison
23. Adlai E. Stevenson	1893-1897	Served President Grover Cleveland
24. Garret A. Hobart	1897-1899	Served President William McKinley
25. Theodore Roosevelt	1901	Served President William McKinley
26. Charles W. Fairbanks	1905-1909	Served President Theodore Roosevelt
27. James Sherman	1909-1912	Served President William H. Taft
28. Thomas Marshall	1913-1921	Served President Woodrow Wilson
29. Calvin Coolidge	1921-1923	Served President Warren Harding
30. Charles G. Dawes	1925-1929	Served President Calvin Coolidge
31. Charles Curtis	1929-1933	Served President Herbert Hoover

32. John Nance Garner	1933-1941	Served President Franklin Roosevelt
33. Henry A. Wallace	1941-1945	Served President Franklin Roosevelt
34. Harry S. Truman	1945	Served President Franklin Roosevelt
35. Alben W. Barkley	1949-1953	Served President Harry Truman
36. Richard M. Nixon	1953-1961	Served President Dwight Eisenhower
37. Lyndon B. Johnson	1961-1963	Served President John Kennedy
38. Hubert H. Humphrey	1965-1969	Served President Lyndon Johnson
39. Spiro T. Agnew	1969-1973	Served President Richard Nixon
40. Gerald R. Ford	1973-1974	Served President Richard Nixon
41. Nelson Rockefeller	1974-1977	Served President Gerald Ford
42. Walter Mondale	1977-1981	Served President James Carter
43. George Bush	1981-1989	Served President Ronald Reagan
44. Dan Quayle	1989-1993	Served President George H.W. Bush
45. Al Gore	1993-2001	Served President Bill Clinton
46. Dick Cheney	2001-	Served President George W. Bush

ALBEN W. BARKLEY

1949-1953 35

Quick Facts About
The Vice Presidency

The Vice Presidential Seal

★ Since 1789, there have been 46 vice presidents serving 43 different presidents... 42 presidents if you only count Grover Cleveland once.

★ The president and vice president are the only United States officials who are elected nationally.

★ The vice president serves as the president, or presiding officer, of the United States Senate.

★ The vice president only casts a vote in the Senate in order to break a tie.

★ Other duties involved in presiding over the Senate include overseeing the final electoral vote count for presidential and vice presidential elections.

★ Should the president die, resign or is removed from office, the vice president succeeds him as the new president.

★ While 44 vice presidents have been elected, two of them never ran for the office and were instead confirmed by Congress. (Gerald Ford, 1973 and Nelson Rockefeller, 1974)

★ From 1788-1800, the presidential candidate who received the second most Electoral College votes was declared the vice president.

★ The vice president and his family live in the Naval Observatory. Originally, the vice president lived in his own private house, but in 1977, Vice President Walter Mondale and his family moved into the renovated Naval Observatory, becoming the first vice president to live in a government supplied house.

★ The 25th Amendment ensured a clear line of succession from vice president to president. Prior to 1967's ratification of the 25th Amendment, it was merely assumed that the vice president would become president upon the death or removal of the president, however, there was no official law granting the vice president the powers of the presidency, thereby assuring a clear line of succession.

★ 33 vice presidents were elected just one time.

★ Only 19 vice presidents were elected for just one term and completed their full four years.

★ Of the 44 elected vice presidents, 29 completed *at least* one full term in office.

★ Only seven vice presidents completed two full terms in office.

★ Of the 44 elected vice presidents, 14 served less than one full term.

★ 16 of the total 46 vice presidents served less than one full term.

★ Of the 46 total vice presidents, 19 failed to serve a complete term:
  – 9 vice presidents replaced their presidents.
  – 7 vice presidents passed away in office.
  – 2 vice presidents resigned from office.
  – 1 vice president finished another's term.

★ It took three vice presidents to complete the 1973-1977 vice presidential term. (Spiro Agnew, Gerald Ford, Nelson Rockefeller)

★ Seven vice presidents were elected for and completed two complete terms:
  – John Adams
  – Daniel Tompkins

- Thomas Marshall
- John Nance Garner
- Richard Nixon
- George Bush
- Al Gore

★ Ten vice presidents won election to two consecutive terms:
- John Adams
- George Clinton
- Daniel Tompkins
- John Calhoun
- Thomas Marshall
- John Nance Garner
- Richard Nixon
- Spiro Agnew
- George Bush
- Al Gore

So You Want To Be Vice President?

James Sherman, like most Vice Presidents, a frustrated golfer.

What are the four requirements in order to be eligible to become vice president?

A person must be 35 years of age, have been born in the United States, must be a current U.S. citizen, and must reside in an American state or territory.

When did the Constitutional Convention approve the office of the Vice Presidency?

On September 6th, 1787, the Constitutional Convention approved the office of the Vice Presidency.

How did the Constitution originally call for the choosing of a vice president?

The Founding Fathers thought that the candidate with the second most electoral votes should become vice president. The founders assumed that the second place vote getter would be the second most qualified, and therefore should be vice president. In 1789 when the Constitution officially became law, there was no "party politics". In addition, "ticket politics", where the presidential candidate selected his running mate, did not exist.

Why was the 12th Amendment instituted in 1804?

Most people agreed that the Electoral College should vote for president and vice president separately. They also agreed the president and vice president should run as a team. The short history of elections showed the potential of having a vice president and president differ with one another. John Adams and Thomas Jefferson did not serve well together as president and vice president. Neither did Jefferson and Aaron Burr.

So what exactly did the 12th amendment do?

Until the 12th Amendment was ratified in 1804, the first place Electoral College vote getter became president and the second place Electoral College vote getter became vice president. The 12th Amendment allowed the Electoral College to vote separately for president and vice president, motivating presidential candidates, and political parties, to run candidates as a team.

Who were the first President and Vice President to run together as a ticket?

In 1804, following the adoption of the 12th Amendment, Thomas Jefferson and George Clinton ran together.

Does the vice president have to be a native born citizen?

Yes.

Is the vice president part of the legislative, executive or judicial branches of office?

Although the vice president is considered part of the executive branch, the constitution clearly leaves that office in limbo as far as which part of the government it truly belongs to. For instance, the vice president is also the President of the U.S. Senate, the chief legislative body.

How many people work for the vice president?

Differs from administration.

What are the legal duties of the vice president of the United States?

The vice president's legal duties as defined by the Constitution are to preside over the Senate, break tie votes, and replace the president upon the president's removal from office.

If the vice president becomes president, does that time spent finishing out his predecessor's term count against his eligibility should he run for re-election?

Yes. The vice president who finishes at the term of a president, is limited to a total of 10 years as president.

The Chief Justice of the Supreme Court gives the Oath of Office to the president, so who gives the oath to the vice president?

Any judge at the discretion of the vice president to be.

Can a president and vice president be from the same state?

No.

Can a president be elected vice president after having served two full terms as president?

While there is no law stating specifically that he can not become a vice president, he cannot succeed to the presidency if needed, due to the 22nd Amendment. This amendment states the President can only serve two full terms or 10 years in office. This then precludes him from being qualified to serve as a vice president.

How can the vice president be removed from office?

According to Article II, Section 4 of the Constitution, "The President, Vice President and all Officers of the United States, shall be removed from Office on Impeachment for, and Conviction of, Treason, Bribery, or other high Crimes and Misdemeanors." The impeachment process occurs in the House of Representatives with a trial and possible conviction, taking place in the Senate.

Who becomes president if the president and vice president are removed from office?

The Speaker of the House.

How many vice presidents have been removed from office?

None.

If the vice-president dies in office, how does a new vice president take office?

The president selects a vice presidential nominee and both the House of Representatives and the United States Senate must approve the selection.

When was the 25th Amendment implemented, and how did it change the presidency and vice presidency?

The 25th amendment was adopted February 10, 1967. With its implementation, the 25th Amendment became final arbitrator of the process of replacement. The major points of the amendment:

- That a vacancy can only be filled once both houses of Congress approve via a majority vote.

- That the president can declare, in writing to the President Pro Tem of the Senate and Speaker of the House, his inability to fulfill his duties, even temporarily, in which case, the vice president assumes the office on an acting basis.

- That in the case of presidential or vice presidential disability, the president or vice president and a majority of principle officers of the executive department, or, another body that Congress may provide, can send written declaration to the Senate Pro Tem and Speaker of the House that the President or Vice President is unable to carry-out his duties.

- That the President can transmit to the Senate Pro Tem and Speaker of the House his ability to resume his duties, unless the vice president and a majority of principle officers of the executive department, or, another body that Congress may provide, transmits another written declaration to the Senate Pro Tem and Speaker of the House stating his inability to carry out his duties. At that time, Congress will decide the issue.

Name the only two vice presidents never elected to office by the voters or the Electoral College.

Gerald Ford and Nelson Rockefeller never ran successfully for national office, but were instead nominated to the vice presidency. Ford was nominated by President Richard Nixon and Rockefeller was nominated by President Gerald Ford.

How long did it take Congress to confirm Nelson Rockefeller as vice president?

In 1974, it took Congress four months to confirm the former Governor of New York, who then served from December 1974 until January 1977.

Name the only vice president never elected by the voters or the Electoral College to become president.

In 1973 Gerald Ford was appointed by President Nixon to replace Vice President Agnew who had resigned. The following year, upon President Nixon's own resignation, Ford became president.

GERALD RUDOLPH FORD

1973 - 1974

40

Which vice president was elected in the Electoral College vote, though the president was not?

John Calhoun was elected vice president in 1824, but no presidential candidate had enough votes in the Electoral College to win election. It then fell to the House of Representatives to decide between Andrew Jackson, John Quincy Adams, William Crawford and Henry Clay. Although Jackson won the popular vote and had the most electoral votes with ninety-nine, the House of Representatives voted for John Quincy Adams as the next president.

Cool Stuff About The Job!

Vice President Charles Dawes shows off his Nobel Peace Prize.

Who was the first vice president to be called the "Veep"?

Alben Barkley received that name from his grandson.

The president lives at The White House, where does the vice president live?

The vice presidential residence is The Naval Observatory, known as The Admiral's House. Formerly it was the official residence of the Chief of Naval operations, however it was turned into the official residence of the vice president in 1974. In 1977, Vice President Walter Mondale became the first vice president to occupy the home.

42

Before the Naval Observatory became the official residence in 1977, where did the vice president and his family live?

Prior to 1977 the vice president was responsible for his own accommodations and stayed in a private residence.

What is the vice president's mailing address?

The White House
1600 Pennsylvania Avenue NW
Washington, DC 20500

What plane does the vice president fly in when he travels?

There are several planes available to the vice president, but whatever plane he flies on, is designated Air Force Two.

Does the vice president have his own seal?

Yes he does, and there have been two official Vice Presidential seals, the first when it was created in 1948 and the second when it was redrawn in 1975. Currently it enjoys the same coat of arms as that of the Presidential seal, with the words, "Seal of the Vice President of the United States" encircling it.

Where are the vice president's offices located?

His main offices are located in the Eisenhower Executive Office Building across the street from the White House, and in the West Wing of the White House itself.

"Hail to the Chief" is played when the president makes an appearance, what song is played upon the vice president's arrival?

Hail Columbia.

Who was the first sitting vice president to appear on a television show?

On August 26th, 1951, Alben Barkley appeared on *"Man of the Week"*.

How does one address the Vice President?

Mr. or Ms. Vice President.

Does the vice president receive two salaries for being both vice president and president of the Senate, or does he get just one?

He receives one salary of $192,600 for being vice president. In addition he gets a $10,000 taxable expense allowance.

How much has the Vice President earned throughout history?

1789-	$5,000
1873-	$10,000
1907-	$12,000
1949-	$30,000
1955-	$35,000
1964-	$43,000
1969-	$62,500
2001-	$171,500
2003-	$192,600

HENRY AGARD WALLACE

1941-1945

33

What type of pension does the vice president receive?

The vice president receives no formal pension other than the standard pension due government employees.

What is the oath of office for the Vice President?

I do solemnly swear that I will support and defend the Constitution of the United States against all enemies foreign and domestic, that I will bear true faith and allegiance to the same: that I take this obligation freely, without any mental reservation or purpose of evasion, and I will well and faithfully discharge the duties of the office on which I am about to enter. So help me God.

What vice president hosted his own television program?

Alben Barkley hosted "Meet The Veep", which was broadcast on NBC for seven months.

How many vice presidents have thrown out the first ball on opening day of the baseball season?

Seven vice presidents have performed the honor 10 times:

- James Sherman, 1912
- Thomas Marshall, 1917, 1920
- Charles Dawes, 1926
- John Nance Garner 1939
- Henry Wallace, 1942, 1944
- Richard Nixon, 1959
- Hubert Humphrey, 1966, 1968

What town in Texas is named after a vice president?

Dallas, Texas was named after George Dallas, who as vice president supported Texas' annexation. Dallas, however, was from Pennsylvania.

What town in Alaska is named after a vice president?

Fairbanks, Alaska is named after Charles Fairbanks who in 1898, before becoming vice president, was appointed to the Joint High Commission to decide the boundary dividing the Alaska Territory from Canada.

Which vice president has the most counties named after him, and where are they?

There are eleven counties named after John Calhoun. They are in the states of Alabama, Arkansas, Florida, Georgia, Illinois, Iowa, Michigan, Mississippi, South Carolina, Texas, and West Virginia.

Which vice president had a county named after him and then had the honor taken away?

King County in Washington State was originally named after William King. However, in 1986 the City Council decided to change its namesake to honor Dr. Martin Luther King, Jr.

The vice president certifies the Electoral College vote and announces the new president. How many vice presidents have been able to announce in Senate chambers that they had become president?

Only four vice presidents were able to announce themselves:
- John Adams in 1796.
- Thomas Jefferson in 1800.
- Martin Van Buren in 1836.
- George H. W. Bush in 1988.

How many vice presidents have had to announce in Senate chambers that they had lost the campaign for president?

Three have had that unhappy chore:
- John Breckinridge declared Abraham Lincoln president in 1860.
- Richard Nixon announced John F. Kennedy as the winner in 1960.
- Al Gore pronounced George H.W. Bush as the next president in 2000.

Which vice president was the first to attend cabinet meetings?

The vice presidency was originally considered a legislative post as much as an executive post, and therefore, many vice presidents aligned themselves with the legislature rather than the executive branch. Thomas Marshall, who served under President Woodrow Wilson starting in 1913, became the first to attend cabinet meetings.

What is the foreign policy role of the vice president?

The president determines the foreign policy role and all other roles performed by the vice president with the exception of his job as President of the Senate.

Which vice president cast the most tie-breaking votes in the Senate?

John Adams did it 29 times.

What vice presidents cast tie-breaking votes in the Senate against the wishes of their presidents?

- In 1802, Aaron Burr cast a tie-breaking vote that sent a Judiciary Act bill back to committee, against President Thomas Jefferson's wishes. The bill was written to repeal the Judiciary Act of 1801, which provided more federal judges on the bench, thereby favoring the Federalist party under President John Adams. The bill eventually did pass the Senate.

- George Clinton cast a tie-breaking vote in 1811 that went against President James Madison's support of legislation renewing the Bank of the United States.

- John Calhoun cast a tie-breaking vote in 1832 against President Andrew Jackson's selection of Martin Van Buren as minister to Britain. The Vice President effectively ended Van Buren's nomination. Jackson, who had been at odds with Calhoun then picked Van Buren to be his running mate in the 1832 election. Calhoun eventually resigned from office. Upon Van Buren's defeat, Senator Thomas Hart Benton said "You have broken a minister, and elected a Vice-President".

How many times did each vice president cast a tie-breaking vote?

- John Adams   29
- Thomas Jefferson   3
- Aaron Burr   3
- George Clinton   11
- Elbridge Gerry   8
- Daniel Tompkins   5
- John Calhoun   28
- Martin Van Buren   4
- Richard Johnson   14
- John Tyler   0
- George Dallas   19
- Millard Fillmore   5
- William King   0
- John Breckinridge   10
- Hannibal Hamlin   7
- Andrew Johnson   0
- Schuyler Colfax   13
- Henry Wilson   1
- William Wheeler   5
- Chester Arthur   3

RICHARD MENTOR JOHNSON

1837 – 1841

- Thomas Hendricks 0
- Levi Morton 4
- Adlai Stevenson 2
- Garret Hobart 1
- Theodore Roosevelt 0
- Charles Fairbanks 0
- James Sherman 4
- Thomas Marshall 10
- Calvin Coolidge 0
- Charles Dawes 2
- Charles Cutis 3
- John Nance Garner 3
- Henry Wallace 4
- Harry Truman 1
- Alben Barkley 7
- Richard Nixon 8
- Lyndon Johnson 0
- Hubert Humphrey 4
- Spiro Agnew 2
- Gerald Ford 0
- Nelson Rockefeller 0
- Walter Mondale 1
- George Bush 7
- Dan Quayle 0
- Al Gore 4
- Dick Cheney 6

CHARLES CURTIS

1929~1933   31

Through May, 2003

Which two vice presidents have been charged with treason?

Aaron Burr and John Breckinridge. Burr was charged with treason for attempting to secede parts of the country from the United States and form its own country with him as President. Breckinridge was charged with treason for abandoning the United States and becoming a general in the Confederate army.

Which two vice presidents were accused of accepting bribes while in office?

Schuyler Colfax and Spiro Agnew.

How many vice presidents have resigned from office?

There have been two vice presidents who have resigned from office.

- John C. Calhoun resigned in 1832 after serving under both John Quincy Adams and Andrew Jackson. In 1832, Calhoun resigned his office, nine weeks before the end of his term. He was later elected to the Senate from South Carolina.

- In 1973, Spiro Agnew resigned his office due to charges of corruption, bribery, and kickbacks while serving as governor of Maryland, as well as a host of charges including income tax evasion by the U.S. Department of Justice.

Vice Presidency: Stepping Stone Or Millstone?

Henry Wallace and Hubert Humphrey often secured the support of labor.

How many vice presidents went directly from the vice presidency to the presidency, either through direct election or due to presidential death or resignation?

13 vice presidents became president while serving in the office of vice president:

- John Adams, 1796.   Direct election.
- Thomas Jefferson, 1800.   Direct election.
- Martin Van Buren, 1836.   Direct election.
- John Tyler, 1841.   Presidential death.
- Millard Fillmore, 1850.   Presidential death.
- Andrew Johnson, 1865.   Presidential death.
- Chester Arthur, 1881.   Presidential death.
- Theodore Roosevelt, 1901. Presidential death.
- Calvin Coolidge, 1923.   Presidential death.
- Harry Truman, 1945.   Presidential death.
- Lyndon Johnson, 1963.   Presidential death.
- Gerald Ford, 1974.   Presidential resignation.
- George Bush, 1988.   Direct election.

GEORGE HERBERT WALKER BUSH

1981-1989

43

How many vice presidents became president due to the death or resignation of the president?

Nine vice presidents succeeded to the office of president without being elected to that office:

- John Tyler, 1841.   Presidential death.
- Millard Fillmore, 1850.   Presidential death.
- Andrew Johnson, 1865.   Presidential death.
- Chester Arthur, 1881.   Presidential death.
- Theodore Roosevelt, 1901.   Presidential death.
- Calvin Coolidge, 1923.   Presidential death.
- Harry Truman, 1945.   Presidential death.
- Lyndon Johnson, 1963.   Presidential death.
- Gerald Ford, 1974.   Presidential resignation.

How many vice presidents were re-elected president after succeeding to the office?

There were four who first won election to the presidency while serving in that office:

- Theodore Roosevelt, 1904
- Calvin Coolidge, 1924
- Harry Truman, 1948
- Lyndon Johnson, 1964

Of the vice presidents who succeed to the presidency due to the death of the president, how many had less than half the term remaining?

Two finished out terms that had less than two years remaining. Calvin Coolidge served from 1923-1925, finishing President Warren Harding's term, and Lyndon Johnson served from 1963-1965, finishing President John F. Kennedy's term.

Which Vice President served the shortest time before becoming president?

John Tyler served merely a month before William Henry Harrison passed away.

How many vice presidents were directly elected president?

Four were directly elected President after serving as Vice President:

- John Adams, 1796.
- Thomas Jefferson, 1800.
- Martin Van Buren, 1836.
- George Bush, 1988.

Who was the youngest vice president to assume the office of president due to the death or resignation of the president?

When Theodore Roosevelt assumed the office of president in 1901 after the assassination of President McKinley, he was 42 years old.

Who was the oldest vice president to assume the office due to the death or resignation of the president?

Harry Truman, who was 60 when he became president in 1945.

Who was the only vice president to serve two full terms as president?

Thomas Jefferson, who was vice president from 1797-1801 under President John Adams, was then elected president in both 1800 and 1804, and served out his complete terms.

Which vice president served for eight days without a president in office?

John Adams served as vice president in 1789 for eight days because George Washington arrived late for the first inauguration.

Who was the first vice president to be nominated to a second consecutive term?

John Adams.

Who was the first vice president to lose his bid for re-election?

In 1840, Vice President Richard Johnson along with President Martin Van Buren lost to William Henry Harrison and John Tyler.

Who is the first vice president to serve as acting president?

In 1985, under the rules of the 25th Amendment, George Bush served as president for eight hours while President Reagan underwent surgery.

Who is the only vice president in the 20th century who was elected to the presidency upon the completion of his vice presidential term?

George Bush, who as Vice President won the presidential election in 1988.

Why have there been more vice presidents than presidents?

Since 1789, there have been 46 different vice presidents and 43 different presidents (counting Cleveland twice). Thomas Jefferson, James Madison, Andrew Jackson, Abraham Lincoln, Ulysses S. Grant, Grover Cleveland and William McKinley had two different vice presidents each, while Franklin Roosevelt had three. The tally has become closer in recent years due to the 25th Amendment as Richard Nixon and Gerald Ford had a total of three vice presidents between them. Also, John Tyler, Millard Fillmore, Andrew Johnson and Chester Arthur never served with a vice president.

How many vice presidents have become president?

14 vice presidents have moved up the political ladder:

- John Adams
- Thomas Jefferson
- Martin Van Buren
- John Tyler
- Millard Fillmore
- Andrew Johnson
- Chester Arthur
- Theodore Roosevelt
- Calvin Coolidge
- Harry Truman
- Lyndon Johnson
- Richard Nixon
- Gerald Ford
- George Bush

HARRY S. TRUMAN

1945   34

How many vice presidents have been elected president?

Nine vice presidents have managed to become president on their own:

- John Adams
- Thomas Jefferson
- Martin Van Buren
- Theodore Roosevelt
- Calvin Coolidge
- Harry Truman
- Lyndon Johnson
- Richard Nixon
- George Bush

Hannibal Hamlin and Henry Wallace share a special distinction. Both were vice presidents to war presidents, both were replaced, and both presidents passed away shortly thereafter, allowing the new vice president to succeed to the presidency. Who were the vice presidents that replaced them?

Andrew Johnson replaced Hannibal Hamlin and Henry Wallace was replaced by Harry Truman.

Who was the only incumbent vice president to run against a sitting president?

Thomas Jefferson when he ran against and defeated John Adams in the election of 1800.

Which vice presidents competed against one another for president in the general election?

- John Adams and Thomas Jefferson in 1800.
- Richard Nixon and Hubert Humphrey in 1968.

Who were the four incumbent vice president's that ran for the presidency, but lost, since 1860?

- John Breckinridge, 1860.
- Richard Nixon, 1960.
- Hubert Humphrey, 1968.
- Al Gore, 2000.

How did Gerald Ford become vice president and president when he was not elected?

Ford was appointed in 1973, by President Richard Nixon to assume the vice presidency when it became vacant upon the resignation of Spiro Agnew, who was force to resign. He was confirmed by the Senate and House, and in 1974, when President Nixon resigned he assumed the presidency.

How many vice presidents were also unsuccessful candidates for the vice presidency?

Nine men have tasted both victory and defeat, while a tenth, James Sherman, died a week before being defeated for re-election.

Aaron Burr	1800 victory 1796 defeat
George Clinton	1804 and 1808 victories 1789, 1792, 1796 defeats
Richard Johnson	1836 victory 1840 defeat

John Tyler	1840 victory
	1836 defeat
Thomas Hendricks	1884 victory
	1876 defeat
Charles Fairbanks	1904 victory
	1916 defeat
James Sherman **	1908 victory
	1912 defeat
Charles Curtis	1928 victory
	1932 defeat
Dan Quayle	1988 victory
	1992 defeat
Walter Mondale	1976 victory
	1980 defeat

** James Sherman was nominated for vice president, but he died before the election. His ticket did lose.

How many unsuccessful candidates for vice president became president?

Only two people have rebounded from failure to ultimate success.

- John Tyler was an unsuccessful vice presidential nominee in 1836, before winning the office in 1840. He then succeeded to the presidency upon the death of President Harrison in 1841.

- Franklin D. Roosevelt ran unsuccessfully for vice president in 1920, and then won the presidency in 1932.

Which 20th century vice presidents secured their parties nomination for president.

Ten 20th century vice presidents were given the chance to be their party's standard-bearer for president:

- Theodore Roosevelt
- Calvin Coolidge
- Harry Truman
- Richard Nixon
- Lyndon Johnson
- Hubert Humphrey
- Gerald Ford
- Walter Mondale
- George Bush
- Al Gore

How many vice presidents were never major party nominees for president?

29 were never a major party candidate for president:

- Elbridge Gerry
- Daniel Tompkins
- John Calhoun
- Richard M. Johnson
- John Tyler
- George Dallas
- William King
- Hannibal Hamlin
- Andrew Johnson
- Schuyler Colfax
- Henry Wilson
- William Wheeler
- Chester Arthur

SCHUYLER COLFAX

1869-1873

17

- Thomas Hendricks
- Levi P. Morton
- Adlai Stevenson
- Garret Hobart
- Charles Fairbanks
- James Sherman
- Thomas Marshall
- Charles Dawes
- Charles Curtis
- John N. Garner
- Henry Wallace
- Alben Barkley
- Spiro Agnew
- Nelson Rockefeller
- Dan Quayle
- Dick Cheney

27

Which vice presidents were not nominated for a second term even though the president they served ran again?

- Aaron Burr was not renominated by Thomas Jefferson in 1804. Burr had killed Secretary of the Treasury Alexander Hamilton in a duel and was later tried, but not convicted, of treason for trying to help parts of the United States secede.

- John C. Calhoun was not renominated by John Quincy Adams in 1828. Instead, Calhoun ran with Andrew Jackson and was victorious, thereby serving his two terms with two different presidents.

- Richard Johnson was not renominated by Martin Van Buren in 1840, but was one of three candidates for vice president running on the Democratic ticket. Along with Johnson were Littleton Waller Tazewell and James Polk. Johnson, however, was recognized as the official nominee.

- Hannibal Hamlin was not renominated by Abraham Lincoln in 1864, and was replaced by Andrew Johnson.

- Schuyler Colfax was not renominated by Ulysses S. Grant in 1872.

- Thomas Hendricks was not renominated by Grover Cleveland in 1888 due to the fact that he had passed away in office in 1885. Cleveland campaigned with Allen Gransberry Thurman in 1888 and was defeated by Benjamin Harrison.

- Levi Morton was not renominated by Benjamin Harrison in 1892, who instead chose Whitelaw Reid as his running mate. Harrison and Reid lost that election to Grover Cleveland and Adlai Stevenson.

- Garret Hobart died in 1899 and therefore was not renominated by William McKinley in 1900.

- Henry Wallace was not renominated by Franklin Roosevelt in 1944, replaced on the ticket by Harry Truman.

Which vice presidents were renominated for a second term but not reelected?

- Though Richard Johnson wasn't renominated by Martin Van Buren in 1840, he still became the official Democratic candidate for the vice presidency in 1840, but he and Van Buren lost to William Henry Harrison and John Tyler.

- Charles Curtis was renominated by Herbert Hoover in 1932, but the pair lost to Franklin Roosevelt and John Nance Garner.

- Walter Mondale ran for re-election with Jimmy Carter in 1980, but they lost to Ronald Reagan and George Bush.

- Dan Quayle got the nod from George Bush to run again in 1992, but they were defeated by Bill Clinton and Al Gore.

Which vice presidents were renominated for a second term and were reelected?

- John Adams was renominated by George Washington, 1792.
- George Clinton was renominated by James Madison, 1808.*
- Daniel D. Tompkins was renominated by James Monroe, 1820.
- John C. Calhoun was renominated by Andrew Jackson 1828.**
- Thomas Marshall was renominated by Woodrow Wilson, 1916.
- John Nance Garner was renominated by Franklin Roosevelt, 1936.
- Richard M. Nixon was renominated by Dwight Eisenhower, 1956.
- Spiro T. Agnew was renominated by Richard Nixon, 1972.
- George Bush was renominated by Ronald Reagan, 1984.
- Al Gore was renominated by Bill Clinton, 1996.

George Clinton had been nominated by Thomas Jefferson in 1804.
**John Calhoun had been vice president for John Quincy Adams in 1824.*

Which vice president was not renominated for a third term?

John Nance Garner. Garner was nominated in 1932 and 1936. In 1940, Roosevelt selected Henry Wallace to serve in Roosevelt's third term.

How many vice presidents were elected to serve two terms under the same president?

Only eight vice presidents have been elected twice with the same president and one of those, Spiro Agnew failed to finish his second term:

- John Adams served under George Washington
- Daniel Tompkins served under James Monroe
- Thomas Marshall served under Woodrow Wilson

- John Nance Garner served under Franklin Roosevelt
- Richard Nixon served under Dwight Eisenhower
- Spiro Agnew served under Richard Nixon
- George Bush served under Ronald Reagan
- Al Gore served under Bill Clinton

How many vice presidents have been elected to and served two full terms?

Seven vice presidents have been able to complete two full four year terms for a total of eight-years:

- John Adams
- Daniel Thompkins
- Thomas Marshall
- John Nance Garner
- Richard Nixon
- George Bush
- Al Gore

Grover Cleveland ran for president three times, winning two non-consecutive terms. Who were his vice presidential candidates in each election?

1885   21

Thomas Hendricks served with Cleveland in1885 before passing away, while Adlai Stevenson was his Vice President from 1893 until 1897. Alan Thurman was defeated along with Cleveland in 1888, although they were the leading vote getters.

How many vice presidents served under Franklin Roosevelt?

He had three:
- John Nance Garner
- Henry Wallace
- Harry Truman

From 1968 through 1977, how many vice presidents were there?

During that 10-year period there were five different vice presidents:
- Hubert Humphrey
- Spiro Agnew
- Gerald Ford
- Nelson Rockefeller
- Walter Mondale

Which vice president announced shortly after being sworn in that he would not seek re-election only to change his mind later, without success?

Schuyler Colfax announced he was not willing to serve two terms. When President U.S. Grant announced he would run again, Colfax campaigned for the office but Henry Wilson was nominated and elected instead.

During the 19th century, which presidents served more years as vice president than president?

None.

Which presidents served more years as vice president than president in the 20th century?

George Bush and Richard Nixon both spent more time as vice president than present. Both of them served two complete terms as vice president. Nixon was forced to resign from office before finishing his second term as President and Bush failed to win re-election to the White House.

What incumbent vice president died just weeks short of the national election?

James Sherman died in 1912, just weeks before the November election. Though he got over 3 million votes, he and William Howard Taft were defeated by Woodrow Wilson and Thomas Marshall.

Who was the first vice president to die in office?

George Clinton in 1812.

Which vice president served the shortest term due to passing away in office?

William King who died after 46 days in office.

Which vice president served the shortest term due to replacing the president?

John Tyler, who replaced William Henry Harrison after just 30 days in office.

Why were there periods of time when the United States did not have a sitting vice president?

Until the 25th amendment, presidents were not required to replace the vice president if the vice president left office, due to death or resignation, and vice presidents who became president upon the president's death, were not required to select a replacement.

How often has the vice presidency been vacant?

From 1789 through 2003, the vice presidency has been vacant for a total of 37 years and 290 days, over the course of 18 administrations.

Seven vice presidents died in office and were not replaced.
Two vice presidents resigned and one of those was not replaced.
Nine vice presidents succeeded to the Presidency, and eight vice presidents were not replaced.

1812	George Clinton passed away in office
1814	Elbridge Gerry passed away in office
1832	John Calhoun resigned in office
1841	John Tyler assumed the presidency
1850	Millard Fillmore assumed the presidency
1853	William King died just days after taking the oath
1865	Andrew Johnson assumed the presidency
1875	Henry Wilson passed away in office.
1881	Chester Arthur assumed the presidency
1885	Thomas Hendricks passed away in office
1899	Garret Hobart passed away in office
1901	Theodore Roosevelt assumed the presidency
1912	James Sherman passed away in office
1923	Calvin Coolidge assumed the presidency
1945	Harry Truman assumed the presidency

1963   Lyndon Johnson assumed the presidency

1973   Spiro Agnew resigned from office

1974   Gerald Ford assumed the presidency

What is the longest period of time that the vice presidency has been vacant?

- The longest consecutive period of time was just short of four years, when John Tyler assumed the presidency after the death of William Henry Harrison, a mere 30 days after being inaugurated.

- There were two extended periods when the office was occupied only for a short period of time. On July 9, 1850, Millard Fillmore assumed the presidency upon the death of Zachary Taylor, leaving the vice presidency vacant until March 4, 1853, when William King took office. King, however, died 46 days later and the office was once again vacant until March 4, 1857, when John Breckinridge took the oath of office, a total of 2,388 vacant days.

- On September 19, 1881, Chester Arthur became president following the assassination of President Garfield, and the office stayed empty until Thomas Hendricks became Grover Cleveland's vice president on March 4, 1885. Unfortunately, Hendricks died on November 25th of that same year and the office was again empty until Levi Morton assumed the role on March 4, 1889, a total of 2,456 days without a vice president.

How many vice presidents returned to the House of Representatives after finishing their term as vice president?

None.

How many vice presidents became Senators after finishing their term as vice president?

6 vice presidents continued their public service as members of the Senate:

- John Calhoun
- John Breckinridge
- Hannibal Hamlin
- Andrew Johnson
- Alben Barkley
- Hubert Humphrey

How many vice presidents became governors after finishing their term as vice president?

Levi Morton was the only vice president to become governor after serving his term, when he took over the New York state house in 1895.

How many vice presidents have been elected to only one term?

33 of the 46 vice presidents were only elected to one term in office:

- Thomas Jefferson   1797-1801
- Aaron Burr   1801-1805
- Elbridge Gerry   1813-1814
- Martin Van Buren   1833-1837
- Richard Johnson   1837-1841
- John Tyler   1841
- George Dallas   1845-1849
- Millard Fillmore   1849-1850

- William R. King   1853
- John Breckinridge   1857-1861
- Hannibal Hamlin   1861-1865
- Andrew Johnson   1865
- Schuyler Colfax   1869-1873
- Henry Wilson   1873-1875
- William Wheeler   1877-1881
- Chester Arthur   1881
- Thomas Hendricks   1885
- Levi P. Morton   1889-1893
- Adlai E. Stevenson   1893-1897
- Garret Hobart   1897-1899
- Theodore Roosevelt   1901
- Charles Fairbanks   1905-1909
- James Sherman   1909-1912
- Calvin Coolidge   1921-1923
- Charles Dawes   1925-1929
- Charles Curtis   1929-1933
- Henry Wallace   1941-1945
- Harry Truman   1945
- Alben Barkley   1949-1953
- Lyndon Johnson   1961-1963
- Hubert Humphrey   1965-1969
- Walter Mondale   1977-1981
- Dan Quayle   1989-1993

How many vice presidents have served completed terms for which they were elected?

28 vice presidents have managed to fulfill their entire term, seven of which completed a full eight years:

- John Adams   Twice
- Thomas Jefferson
- Aaron Burr
- George Clinton
- Daniel Tompkins   Twice
- John C. Calhoun
- Martin Van Buren
- Richard Johnson
- George Dallas
- John Breckinridge
- Hannibal Hamlin
- Schuyler Colfax
- William Wheeler
- Levi Morton
- Adlai Stevenson
- Charles Fairbanks
- Thomas Marshall   Twice
- Charles Dawes
- Charles Curtis
- John Nance Garner   Twice
- Henry Wallace
- Alben Barkley
- Richard Nixon   Twice
- Hubert Humphrey
- Walter Mondale
- George Bush   Twice
- Dan Quayle
- Al Gore   Twice

LEVI PARSONS MORTON

1889~1893

22

Which vice presidents failed to complete their term in office, and why?

- George Clinton — Died in office
- Elbridge Gerry — Died in office
- John Calhoun — Resigned
- John Tyler — Assumed Presidency
- Millard Fillmore — Assumed Presidency
- William R. King — Died in office
- Andrew Johnson — Assumed Presidency
- Henry Wilson — Died in office
- Chester Arthur — Assumed Presidency
- Thomas Hendricks — Died in office
- Garret Hobart — Died in office
- Theodore Roosevelt — Assumed Presidency
- James Sherman — Died in office
- Calvin Coolidge — Assumed Presidency
- Harry Truman — Assumed Presidency
- Lyndon Johnson — Assumed Presidency
- Spiro Agnew — Resigned
- Gerald Ford — Assumed Presidency

Which vice president's held other elected offices after serving as vice president, and what office did they hold?

- John Adams — Elected President in 1796
- Thomas Jefferson — Elected President in 1800
- John Calhoun — Elected to Senate in 1832
- Martin Van Buren — Elected President in 1836
- Richard M. Johnson — Elected to State Legislature, 1850
- John Tyler — Elected to Confederate House of Representatives, 1862
- Hannibal Hamlin — Elected to Senate in 1869
- Andrew Johnson — Elected to Senate in 1875
- Levi Morton — Elected Governor in 1895
- Theodore Roosevelt — Elected President in 1904
- Calvin Coolidge — Elected President in 1924
- Harry Truman — Elected President in 1948
- Alben Barkley — Elected to Senate in 1955
- Lyndon Johnson — Elected President in 1964
- Richard Nixon — Elected President in 1968
- Hubert Humphrey — Elected to Senate in 1970
- George H.W. Bush — Elected President in 1988

YES, We're Going To A Party, Party!

Dan Quayle never could spell the word potato.
But he was quite an athlete.

Have there been more Democratic or Republican vice presidents?

There have been 20 Republican vice presidents and 17 Democratic.

Who was the first Republican to win the vice presidency?

Hannibal Hamlin of Maine in 1860.

Who were the Republican vice presidents?

- Hamlin
- Colfax
- Wilson
- Wheeler
- Arthur
- Morton
- Hobart
- T. Roosevelt
- Fairbanks
- Sherman
- Coolidge
- Dawes
- Curtis
- Nixon
- Agnew
- Ford
- Rockefeller
- Bush
- Quayle
- Cheney

1881

20

Who was the first Democrat to win the vice presidency?

Martin Van Buren of New York in 1832.

Who were the Democratic vice presidents?

- Van Buren
- R. Johnson
- Dallas
- King
- Breckinridge
- Johnson
- Hendricks
- Stevenson
- Marshall
- Garner
- Wallace
- Truman
- Barkley
- L.B. Johnson
- Humphrey
- Mondale
- Gore

8

Which vice president was the Democratic running mate of a Republican president?

Andrew Johnson, a southerner and a Democrat, was choosen in 1864 by Abraham Lincoln, a Republican, in order to balance the ticket.

Of the first seven vice presidents, six of them were from the Democratic-Republican party. Name the vice president that was not from that party.

John Adams, the first vice president, who served under George Washington, was a Federalist.

Who was the only Federalist to win the vice presidency?

John Adams of Massachusetts in 1788.

Who was the first Whig to win the vice presidency?

John Tyler of Virginia in 1840.

How many Democratic-Republicans have been vice president?

From 1796 till 1828 all six vice presidents were members of the Democratic-Republican party, however in 1828, Vice President John Calhoun switched to the Democratic party and the Democratic-Republican party was disbanded with the defeat of President John Quincy Adams.

- Thomas Jefferson
- Aaron Burr
- George Clinton
- Elbridge Gerry
- Daniel Tompkins
- John Calhoun

How many other parties besides Democrats and Republicans, have had members elected vice president?

Three:

- Federalist – Adams
- Democratic-Republican – Jefferson, Burr, Clinton, Gerry, Tompkins & Calhoun
- Whig – Tyler & Fillmore

Who were the first president and vice president to be from separate political parties?

Vice President Thomas Jefferson of the Democratic-Republican party was elected in 1796 to serve with President John Adams, a Federalist.

Who was the only future Vice President ever to give the keynote address at a national political convention?

Alben Barkley gave the keynote address at the Democratic conventions in 1936 and 1948. Later at the 1948 convention he was nominated to be the vice presidential candidate.

When Thomas Eagleton resigned the Democratic vice presidential nomination in 1972, who replaced him?

Sargent Shriver.

How many vice presidential debates have there been and who participated?

Through the 2000 election, there have been six vice presidential debates:

- Walter Mondale debated Bob Dole, 1976
- George Bush debated Geraldine Ferraro, 1984
- Dan Quayle debated Lloyd Bentsen, 1988
- Al Gore debated Dan Quayle, 1992
- Al Gore debated Jack Kemp, 1996
- Dick Cheney debated Joe Lieberman, 2000

Which sitting vice president ran against the president he was serving with a presidential running mate from a different party?

John Calhoun accepted John Quincy Adams offer to be his vice presidential candidate in 1824. When Andrew Jackson offered Calhoun the number two spot in the 1828 election, he accepted and won re-election with Jackson against Adams.

Who was the first man to receive a nomination for vice president and decline it?

John Langdon of New Hampshire received the Democratic-Republican nomination to run with President James Madison in 1812. Langdon, 71 years old at the time, declined the nomination because of his advanced age. Elbridge Gerry received the next nomination, accepted the position, and after winning the election, died in office in November of 1814. Lyndon lived until 1819.

ELBRIDGE GERRY

1813~1814 5

64

Which major party candidate lost the most elections for vice president?

Rufus King, who was defeated in 1804 and again in 1808.

Which vice presidents ran for president on a third party ticket?

- Martin Van Buren ran for President on the Free-Soil party ticket in 1848.
- Millard Fillmore ran for President on the Know Nothings ticket in 1856.
- John Breckinridge ran for President on the Democratic parties pro slavery wing ticket in 1860.
- Theodore Roosevelt ran for President on the Bull Moose ticket in1912.
- Henry Wallace ran for President on the Progressive Party ticket in 1948.

Who has been the losing nominee for vice president in each election?

1789   John Jay, New York, Federalist

1792   George Clinton, New York, Democratic-Republican
Thomas Jefferson, Virginia, Democratic-Republican
Aaron Burr, New York, Democratic-Republican

1796   Thomas Pinckney, South Carolina, Federalist
Aaron Burr, New York, Democratic-Republican
Samuel Adams, Federalist

1800   Charles Pinckney, South Carolina, Federalist

1804   Rufus King, New York, Federalist

1808   Rufus King, New York, Federalist

1812   Jared Ingersoll, Pennsylvania, Federalist

1816   John Howard, Maryland, Federalist

1820   No Losers

1824   Nathan Sanford, New York, Democratic-Republican
        Nathaniel Macon, North Carolina, Democratic-Republican

1828   Richard Rush, Pennsylvania, Federalist/National Republican

1832   John Sergeant, Pennsylvania, National Republican

1836   John Tyler, Virginia, Whig
        Francis Granger, New York, Whig
        William Smith, South Carolina, Whig

1840   Richard M. Johnson, Kentucky, Democrat

1844   Theodore Frelinghuysen, New Jersey, Whig

1848   William Orlando Butler, Kentucky, Democrat
        Charles Francis Adams, Massachusetts, Free Soil

1852   William Graham, North Carolina, Whig

1856   William Dayton, New Jersey, Republican
        Andrew Donelson, Tennessee, American

1860   Joseph Lane, Democrat, Oregon, Southern Democrat
        Edward Everett, Massachusetts, Constitutional Union
        Herschel Johnson, Georgia, Northern Democrat

1864   George Pendleton, Ohio, Democrat

1868   Frank Blair, Missouri, Democrat

1872   B. Grantz Brown, Missouri, Democrat

1876   Thomas A. Hendricks, Indiana, Democrat

1880   William H. English, Indiana, Democrat

1884   John A. Logan, Illinois, Republican

1888   Allen G. Thurman, Ohio, Democrat

1892   Whitelaw Reid, New York, Republican

1896	Arthur Sewall, Maine, Democrat
	Thomas Watson, Georiga, Democrat
1900	Adlai Stevenson, Illinois, Democrat
1904	Henry G. Davis, West Virginia, Democrat
1908	John W. Kern, Indiana, Democrat
1912	Hiram Johnson, California, Progressive
	James S. Sherman, New York, Republican
	Nicholas M. Butler, New York, Republican
1916	Charles W. Fairbanks, Indiana, Republican
1920	Franklin D. Roosevelt, New York, Democrat
1924	Charles W. Bryan, Nebraska, Democrat
	Burton K. Wheeler, Montana, Progressive
1928	Joseph T. Robinson, Arkansas, Democrat
1932	Charles Curtis, Kansas, Republican
1936	Frank Knox, Illinois, Republican
1940	Charles L. McNary, Oregon, Republican
1944	John Bricker, Ohio, Republican
1948	Earl Warren, California, Republican
	Fielding Wright, State's Rights Democrat
1952	John Sparkman, Alabama, Democrat
1956	Estes Kefauver, Tennesse, Democrat
1960	Henry Cabot Lodge, Massachusetts, Republican
1964	William Miller, New York, Republican
1968	Edmund Muskie, Maine, Democrat
	Curtis Lemay, Ohio, American Independent
1972	Thomas Eagleton, Missouri, Democrat
	Sargent Shriver, Maryland, Democrat
1976	Bob Dole, Kansas, Republican

1980	Walter Mondale, Minnesota, Democrat
1984	Geraldine Ferraro, New York, Democrat
1988	Lloyd Bensten, Texas, Democrat
1992	J. Danforth Quayle, Indiana, Republican James Stockdale, Independent
1996	Jack Kemp, New York, Republican
2000	Joe Lieberman, Connecticut, Democrat

Qualifications.
There Are
Qualifications, Right?

How many vice presidents have attended college?

34 vice presidents have attended college.

Which vice president never attended one day of school and was taught to read and write by his wife?

Andrew Johnson.

How many vice presidents served in the Continental Congress before becoming vice president?

Four vice presidents were members of the Continental Congress:
- John Adams
- Thomas Jefferson
- Aaron Burr
- Elbridge Gerry

How many vice presidents were never members of Congress before becoming vice president?

13 vice presidents never served in the House of Representatives or the Senate before their term as vice president:
- John Adams
- Thomas Jefferson
- George Clinton
- Daniel Tompkins
- Chester Arthur
- Garret Hobart
- Theodore Roosevelt
- Thomas Marshall

- Calvin Coolidge
- Charles Dawes
- Henry Wallace
- Spiro Agnew
- Nelson Rockefeller

How many vice presidents served in the House of Representatives but not the Senate before becoming vice president?

11 vice presidents started in the lower house of the Congress:

- Gerry
- Fillmore
- Colfax
- Wheeler
- Morton
- Stevenson
- Sherman
- Garner
- Ford
- Bush
- Cheney

How many vice presidents served only in the U.S. Senate before becoming vice president?

Eight vice presidents only served in the upper house of the Congress:

- Aaron Burr
- Martin Van Buren
- George Dallas
- Henry Wilson

- Charles Fairbanks
- Harry Truman
- Hubert Humphrey
- Walter Mondale

How many vice presidents served in both the House of Representatives and the U.S. Senate before becoming vice president?

14 vice presidents served in both houses of the Congress:

- John Calhoun
- Richard Johnson
- John Tyler
- William King
- John Breckinridge
- Hannibal Hamlin
- Andrew Johnson
- Thomas Hendricks
- Charles Curtis
- Alben Barkley
- Richard Nixon
- Lyndon Baines Johnson
- Dan Quayle
- Al Gore

How many vice presidents were members of Congress before becoming vice president?

33 served in either the House of Representatives or the Senate before their term as vice president:

- Aaron Burr
- Elbridge Gerry

- John Calhoun
- Martin Van Buren
- Richard Johnson
- John Tyler
- George Dallas
- Millard Fillmore
- William King
- John Breckinridge
- Hannibal Hamlin
- Andrew Johnson
- Schuyler Colfax
- Henry Wilson
- William Wheeler
- Thomas Hendricks
- Levi Morton
- Adlai Stevenson
- Charles Fairbanks
- James Sherman
- Charles Curtis
- John Nance Garner
- Harry Truman
- Alben Barkley
- Richard Nixon
- Lyndon Johnson
- Hubert Humphrey
- Gerald Ford
- Walter Mondale
- George Bush
- Dan Quayle
- Al Gore
- Dick Cheney

MILLARD FILLMORE

1842~1850

12

How many vice presidents served in the U.S. Senate?

22 were elected to the U.S. Senate:

Aaron Burr	1791-1797	(Elected to One term)
John Calhoun	1832-1843; 1845-50	
Martin Van Buren	1821-1829	(Elected to Two terms)
Richard Johnson	1819-1829	(Elected to Two terms)
John Tyler	1828-1841	(Elected to Two terms)
George Dallas	1831-1833	(Elected to One term)
William R. King	1819-1844; 1848-52	(Elected to Six terms)
John Breckinridge	1861	(Elected to One term)
Hannibal Hamlin	1848-1861; 1869-1881	(Elected to Five terms)
Andrew Johnson	1857-1862; 1875-1885	(Elected to Two terms)
Henry Wilson	1855-1873	(Elected to Four terms)
Thomas Hendricks	1863-1869	(Elected to One term)
Charles Fairbanks	1897-1905	(Elected to Two terms)
Charles Curtis	1907-1913; 1915-1929	(Elected to Five terms)

Curtis was elected on the same day to fill a seat and assume the seat for its full term.

Harry Truman	1935-1945	(Elected to two terms)
Alben Barkley	1927-1949; 1955-1956	(Elected to Five terms)
Richard Nixon	1951-1953	(Elected to One Term)
Lyndon Johnson	1949-1961	(Elected to Two terms)
Hubert Humphrey	1949-1964; 1971-1978	(Elected to Five terms)
Walter Mondale	1964-1976	(Elected to Two terms)
Dan Quayle	1981-1989	(Elected to Two Terms)
Al Gore	1985-1993	(Elected to Two Terms)

How many vice presidents served as governors before becoming vice president?

14 vice presidents served as the chief executives of their states:

- Thomas Jefferson   Virginia
- George Clinton   New York

- Elbridge Gerry — Massachusetts
- Daniel Tompkins — New York
- Martin Van Buren — New York
- John Tyler — Virginia
- Hannibal Hamlin — Maine
- Andrew Johnson — Tennessee
- Thomas Hendricks — Indiana
- Theodore Roosevelt — New York
- Thomas Marshall — Indiana
- Calvin Coolidge — Massachusetts
- Spiro Agnew — Maryland
- Nelson Rockefeller — New York

Which vice president had been elected Governor and Lieutenant Governor of New York at the same time?

George Clinton was on the New York ballot for both governor and lieutenant governor and after winning both elections, kept both jobs.

Have any vice presidents ever served as Speakers of the House?

Schuyler Colfax was the Speaker from 1863 until 1869, and John Nance Garner held the position from 1931-1933.

Which vice presidents were Senate Majority Leaders?

Three vice presidents held that title, the first being Charles Curtis who held the title from 1924 till 1929 when he became Herbert Hoover's vice president. Alben Barkley was the Majority Leader from 1937 until becoming Truman's vice president in 1947, and the last was Lyndon Johnson, who served in that position from 1955 until his election with John Kennedy in 1961.

Which vice presidents were Senate Minority Leaders?

Both Alben Barkley and Lyndon Johnson were Senate Minority Leaders for two years, until their party won control of the Senate making them Majority leaders.

Since 1928, only two Democratic vice presidential nominees did not serve in Congress at any time in their careers. Who were they?

Sargent Shriver and Henry Wallace.

Who is the first vice president to have been the Chief of Staff and Secretary of Defense in two different administrations?

Dick Cheney served as Chief of Staff to President Gerald Ford in 1975 and Secretary of Defense to President George H. W. Bush from 1989-1993.

Besides a political career what was the primary occupation of every vice president?

- John Adams   Lawyer
- Thomas Jefferson   Lawyer
- Aaron Burr   Lawyer
- George Clinton   Lawyer
- Elbridge Gerry   Lawyer

- Daniel Tompkins   Lawyer
- John C. Calhoun   Lawyer
- Martin Van Buren   Lawyer
- Richard Johnson   Lawyer
- John Tyler   Lawyer
- George Dallas   Lawyer
- Millard Fillmore   Lawyer
- William King   Lawyer
- John Breckinridge   Lawyer
- Hannibal Hamlin   Lawyer
- Andrew Johnson   Tailor
- Schuyler Colfax   Business
- Henry Wilson   Business
- William Wheeler   Lawyer
- Chester Arthur   Lawyer
- Thomas Hendricks   Lawyer
- Levi Morton   Business
- Adlai Stevenson   Lawyer
- Garret Hobart   Lawyer
- Theodore Roosevelt   Business
- Charles Fairbanks   Lawyer
- James Sherman   Lawyer
- Thomas Marshall   Lawyer
- Calvin Coolidge   Lawyer
- Charles Dawes   Banker
- Charles Curtis   Lawyer
- John Nance Garner   Lawyer
- Henry Wallace   Writer
- Harry Truman   Farmer
- Alben Barkley   Lawyer
- Richard Nixon   Lawyer

CHARLES WARREN FAIRBANKS

1905~1909

26

- Lyndon Baines Johnson   Teacher
- Hubert Humphrey   Pharmacist
- Spiro Agnew   Lawyer
- Gerald Ford   Lawyer
- Nelson Rockefeller   Business
- Walter Mondale   Lawyer
- George Bush   Business
- Dan Quayle   Lawyer
- Al Gore   Business
- Dick Cheney   Business

Not Just
The Same Old Joe

William King, the only bachelor vice president, was a political leader in the U.S. House and Senate for many years.

Who was the only Native American Indian vice president?

Charles Curtis.

Who was the first black vice presidential candidate to stand for election?

Frederick Douglass ran for vice president in 1872 as a candidate of the Equal Rights Party. His presidential running mate was Victoria Claflin Woodhull.

Who was the first black candidate to be nominated for vice president from a major political party?

At the 1880 Republican convention, Blanche Kelso Bruce, a Senator from Mississippi, received eleven votes in balloting, but did not win the nomination. The nomination for vice president that year went to Chester Arthur. The Republicans won the election and Arthur eventually became president upon the death of James Garfield in 1881.

Who was the first woman to ever become a nominee for vice president?

In 1884, Marietta Lizzie Bell Stow from California, became the vice presidential nominee for the Equal Rights Party.

Who was the first female vice presidential candidate to receive an electoral vote and when?

On January 6, 1973, Roger L. MacBride cast his vote for Theodora Nathan of Oregon.

Who was the first woman vice president nominee on a major ticket?

Geraldine Ferraro ran with Walter Mondale on the 1984 Democratic ticket, which was defeated by Ronald Reagan and George Bush.

Who are all of the women vice presidential candidates?

Women's names have appeared on the ballot as vice presidential candidates 44 times:

- Marietta Lizzie Bell Stow, Equal Rights Party, 1884. Represented California.

- Marie Caroline Brehm, Prohibition Party, 1924. Represented California.

- Florence Garvin, National Greenback Party, 1936. Represented Rhode Island.

- Grace Carlson, Socialist Workers Party, 1948. Represented Minnesota.

- Charlotta Bass, Progressive Party and American Labor Party, 1952. Represented New York.

- Myra Tanner Weiss, Socialist Workers Party, 1952. Represented New York.

- Georgia Cozzini, Socialist Labor Party, 1956. Represented Wisconsin.

- Myra Tanner Weiss, Socialist Workers Party, 1956. Represented New York.

- Ann Marie Yezo, American Third Party, 1956. Represented New Jersey.

- Georgia Cozzini, Socialist Labor Party, 1960. Represented Wisconsin.

- Myra Tanner Weiss, Socialist Workers Party, 1960. Represented New York.

- Judith Mage, Peace and Freedom Party, 1968. Represented New York.

- Theodora Nathan, Libertarian Party, 1972. Represented Oregon.

- Genevieve Gunderson, Socialist Labor Party, 1972. Represented Minnesota.

- Willie Mae Reid, Socialist Labor Party, 1976. Represented California.

- Constance Blomen, Socialist Labor Party, 1976. Represented Massachusetts.

- Angela Davis, Communist Party, 1980. Represented California.

- Carroll Driscoll, Right to Life Party, 1980. Represented New Jersey.

- Diane Drufenbrock, Socialist Party, 1980. Represented Wisconsin.

- LaDonna Harris, Citizens Party, 1980. Represented New Mexico.

- Ellen McCormack, Right to Life Party, 1980. Represented New York.

- Eileen Shearer, American Independent Party, 1980. Represented California.

- Matilde Zimmerman, Socialist Workers Party, 1980. Represented New York.

- Angela Davis, Communist Party, 1984. Represented California.

- Geraldine Ferraro, Democratic Party, 1984. Represented New York.

- Andrea Gonzalez, Socialist Workers Party, 1984. Represented New Jersey.

- Gloria La Riva, Workers World Party, 1984. Represented California.

- Nancy Ross, Independent Alliance Party, 1984.

- Maureen Salaman, Populist Party, 1984.

- Joan Andrews, Right to Life Party, 1988. Represented Ohio.

- Joyce Dattner, New Alliance Party, 1988. Represented New York.

- Kathleen Mickells, Socialist Workers Party, 1988. Represented West Virginia.

- Gloria La Riva, Workers World Party, 1988. Represented California.

- Barbara Garson, Socialist Party, 1992.

- Willa Mae Reid, Socialist Workers Party, 1992.

- Winona Laduke, Green Party, 1996. Represented Minnesota.

- Gloria La Riva, Workers World Party, 1996. Represented California.

- Rachel Bubar Kelly, Prohibition Party, 1996. Represented Illinois.

- Kate McClatchy, Peace and Freedom Party, 1996.

- Laura Garza, Socialist Workers Party, 1996.

- Margaret Trowe, Socialist Party, 2000. Represented Iowa.

- Winona Laduke. Green Party, 2000. Represented Minnesota.

- Gloria La Riva, Workers World Party, 2000. Represented California.

- Mary Cal Hollis. Socialist Party, 2000.

What are the religious affiliations of each vice president?

- John Adams.   Unitarian
- Thomas Jefferson   Unknown
- Aaron Burr   Presbyterian
- George Clinton   Dutch Reformed
- Elbridge Gerry   Episcopalian
- Daniel Tompkins   Presbyterian
- John C. Calhoun   Unknown
- Martin Van Buren   Dutch Reformed
- Richard Johnson   Unknown
- John Tyler   Episcopalian
- George Dallas   Unknown
- Millard Fillmore   Unitarian
- William King   Unknown
- John Breckinridge   Presbyterian
- Hannibal Hamlin   Unknown
- Andrew Johnson   Unknown
- Schuyler Colfax   Unknown
- Henry Wilson   Congregationalist
- William Wheeler   Presbyterian
- Chester Arthur   Episcopalian
- Thomas Hendricks   Episcopalian
- Levi Morton   Protestant
- Adlai Stevenson   Unknown
- Garret Hobart   Unknown
- Theodore Roosevelt   Dutch Reformed
- Charles Fairbanks   Unknown
- James Sherman   Reformed
- Thomas Marshall   Unknown

- Calvin Coolidge   Congregationalist
- Charles Dawes   Unknown
- Charles Curtis   Unknown
- John Nance Garner   Unknown
- Henry Wallace   Presbyterian
- Harry Truman   Baptist
- Alben Barkley   Methodist
- Richard Nixon   Quaker
- Lyndon Baines Johnson   Disciples of Christ
- Hubert Humphrey   Congregationalist
- Spiro Agnew   Episcopalian
- Gerald Ford   Episcopalian
- Nelson Rockefeller   Baptist
- Walter Mondale   Methodist
- George Bush   Episcopalian
- Dan Quayle   "Interdenominational" Fundamentalist
- Al Gore   Baptist
- Dick Cheney   Methodist

College Daze

Andrew Johnson learned to read and write from his wife, Eliza.

What year did the most vice presidential candidates receive Electoral College votes in one election?

In 1872 nine different candidates received electoral votes:

- Henry Wilson   286 (winner)
- B. Gratz Brown   47
- NP Banks   1
- George Julian   5
- Alfred Colquit   5
- John Palmer   3
- Thomas Bramlette   3
- William Groesbeck   1
- Willis Machen   1

Who is the only vice president to have received Electoral College votes for vice president in five different elections?

George Clinton received Electoral College votes for vice president in 1789, 1792, 1796, 1804, 1808.

Which vice president received the fewest electoral votes in winning the Vice Presidency?

George Clinton received 113 electoral votes in the 1808 election as he and James Madison won the election.

Which vice president received the most electoral votes in winning the vice presidency?

George Bush received 525 electoral votes in the 1984 election. The Reagan-Bush ticket carried every state except Minnesota and the District of Columbia.

Which vice presidential nominee received the most electoral votes while losing the election?

Joseph Lieberman received 266 electoral votes in the 2000 election. George W. Bush and Dick Cheney defeated Al Gore and Joseph Lieberman.

Which major party vice presidential nominee received the fewest electoral votes in losing his bid for the vice presidency?

Frank Knox received just eight electoral votes in the 1936 election as Franklin Roosevelt and John Nance Garner defeated Alf Landon and Knox, carrying ever state except for Maine and Vermont.

JOHN NANCE GARNER

1933 - 1941

32

So Where Are You From, Buddy?

Thomas Jefferson and George Clinton share a quiet moment.

What state has produced the most vice presidents?

New York has been considered the home state of 11 vice presidents upon their taking the oath of office.

- Aaron Burr
- George Clinton
- Daniel Tompkins
- Martin Van Buren
- Millard Fillmore
- William Wheeler
- Chester Arthur
- Levi Morton
- Theodore Roosevelt
- James Sherman
- Nelson Rockefeller

In which states have the most vice presidents been born?

- New York   (8)
- Kentucky   (5)
- Massachusetts   (3)
- Ohio   (3)
- Vermont   (3)
- New Jersey   (2)
- Indiana   (2)
- Maine   (2)
- North Carolina   (2)
- Nebraska   (2)
- Virginia   (2)
- Texas   (1)
- California   (1)

- Iowa   (1)
- Kansas   (1)
- Maryland   (1)
- Minnesota   (1)
- Missouri   (1)
- New Hampshire   (1)
- Pennsylvania   (1)
- South Carolina   (1)
- South Dakota   (1)
- Washington, D.C.   (1)

Why has the state of Indiana been referred to as the "Mother of Vice Presidents"?

During the 48-year period from 1868 until 1916, 10 of the major party vice presidential nominees had been from Indiana.

How many vice presidents have been born in California?

One, Richard Nixon.

Which states have most often been the official residence of the vice president while in office?

New York	(11)
Indiana	(5)
Massachusetts	(4)
Kentucky	(3)
Texas	(3)
Illinois	(2)
Tennessee	(2)

Minnesota	(2)
Virginia	(2)
California	(1)
Iowa	(1)
Kansas	(1)
Michigan	(1)
New Jersey	(1)
Maryland	(1)
Missouri	(1)
Pennsylvania	(1)
South Carolina	(1)
Alabama	(1)
Wyoming	(1)
Maine	(1)

In which state was each vice president born?

- John Adams — Massachusetts
- Thomas Jefferson — Virginia
- Aaron Burr — New Jersey
- George Clinton — New York
- Elbridge Gerry — Massachusetts
- Daniel Tompkins — New York
- John C. Calhoun — South Carolina
- Martin Van Buren — New York
- Richard Johnson — Kentucky
- John Tyler — Virginia
- George Dallas — Pennsylvania
- Millard Fillmore — New York
- William King — North Carolina
- John Breckinridge — Kentucky
- Hannibal Hamlin — Maine

- Andrew Johnson   North Carolina
- Schuyler Colfax   New York
- Henry Wilson   New Hampshire
- William Wheeler   New York
- Chester Arthur   Vermont
- Thomas Hendricks   Ohio
- Levi Morton   Vermont
- Adlai Stevenson   Kentucky
- Garret Hobart   New Jersey
- Theodore Roosevelt   New York
- Charles Fairbanks   Ohio
- James Sherman   New York
- Thomas Marshall   Indiana
- Calvin Coolidge   Vermont
- Charles Dawes   Ohio
- Charles Curtis   Kansas
- John Nance Garner   Kentucky
- Henry Wallace   Iowa
- Harry Truman   Missouri
- Alben Barkley   Kentucky
- Richard Nixon   California
- Lyndon Baines Johnson   Texas
- Hubert Humphrey   South Dakota
- Spiro Agnew   Maryland
- Gerald Ford   Nebraska
- Nelson Rockefeller   Maine
- Walter Mondale   Minnesota
- George Bush   Massachusetts
- Dan Quayle   Indiana
- Al Gore   Washington D.C.
- Dick Cheney   Nebraska

Which states are listed as the official resident of each vice president while in office?

- John Adams.   Massachusetts
- Thomas Jefferson   Virginia
- Aaron Burr   New York
- George Clinton   New York
- Elbridge Gerry   Massachusetts
- Daniel Tompkins   New York
- John C. Calhoun   South Carolina
- Martin Van Buren   New York
- Richard Johnson   Kentucky
- John Tyler   Virginia
- George Dallas   Pennsylvania
- Millard Fillmore   New York
- William King   Alabama
- John Breckinridge   Kentucky
- Hannibal Hamlin   Maine
- Andrew Johnson   Tennessee
- Schuyler Colfax   Indiana
- Henry Wilson   Massachusetts
- William Wheeler   New York
- Chester Arthur   New York
- Thomas Hendricks   Indiana
- Levi Morton   New York
- Adlai Stevenson   Illinois
- Garret Hobart   New Jersey
- Theodore Roosevelt   New York
- Charles Fairbanks   Indiana
- James Sherman   New York
- Thomas Marshall   Indiana
- Calvin Coolidge   Massachusetts

- Charles Dawes   Illinois
- Charles Curtis   Kansas
- John Nance Garner   Texas
- Henry Wallace   Iowa
- Harry Truman   Missouri
- Alben Barkley   Kentucky
- Richard Nixon   California
- Lyndon Baines Johnson   Texas
- Hubert Humphrey   Minnesota
- Spiro Agnew   Maryland
- Gerald Ford   Michigan
- Nelson Rockefeller   New York
- Walter Mondale   Minnesota
- George Bush   Texas
- Dan Quayle   Indiana
- Al Gore   Tennessee
- Dick Cheney   Wyoming

How many states have never been the birthplace or official residence of a vice president?

23 states have never had a direct connection to a vice president:

- Alaska
- Arizona
- Arkansas
- Colorado
- Connecticut
- Delaware
- Florida
- Georgia
- Hawaii
- Idaho

- Louisiana
- Mississippi
- Montana
- Nevada
- New Mexico
- North Dakota
- Oklahoma
- Oregon
- Rhode Island
- Utah
- Washington
- West Virginia
- Wisconsin

Coming And Going

Schuyler Colfax and Spiro Agnew were accued of taking bribes in their political careers.

In which month were the most vice presidents born?

October with seven.

- Chester Arthur, 5th, 1829
- Henry Wallace, 7th, 1888
- Richard Johnson, 17th, 1780
- John Adams, 19th, 1735
- Adlai Stevenson, 23rd, 1835
- James Sherman, 24th, 1855
- Theodore Roosevelt, 27th, 1858

Which month has seen the most vice presidential deaths?

November with eight.

- Elbridge Gerry, 23rd, 1814
- Richard Johnson, 19th, 1850
- Henry Wilson, 22nd, 1875
- Chester Arthur, 18th, 1886
- Thomas Hendricks, 25th, 1885
- Garret Hobart, 21st, 1899
- John Nance Garner, 7th, 1967
- Henry Wallace, 18th, 1965

Who was the oldest vice president to be elected to the office?

Alben Barkley, who was Harry Truman's running mate in 1948, was 71 when he assumed the office.

Who was the youngest vice president to be elected to the office?

John Breckinridge was 36 when he assumed office in 1857, just one year over the required age.

What is the average age for vice presidents when assuming the office?

The average age upon becoming vice president is 53.

What is the average age of death for vice presidents?

The average vice president has been 73 upon his death.

What is the average length of service for a vice president?

More than three years but less than four.

Who was the oldest vice presidential nominee for a major party?

When Henry Gassaway Davis was nominated at the 1904 Democratic convention, he was 80 years of age. He and presidential candidate Alton Parker lost to the ticket of Theodore Roosevelt and Charles Fairbanks.

Which vice presidents became president due to assassination?

- Andrew Johnson assumed the Presidency upon Abraham Lincoln's assassination in 1865.

- Chester Arthur assumed the Presidency upon James Garfield's assassination in 1881.

- Theodore Roosevelt assumed the Presidency upon William McKinley's assassination in 1901.

- Lyndon Johnson assumed the Presidency upon John F. Kennedy's assassination in 1963.

Which three vice presidents share the same birthday?

Hannibal Hamlin, Charles Dawes and Lyndon Johnson were all born on August 27th.

Who is the only vice president born in September?

Thomas Hendricks, September 7th, 1819.

CALVIN COOLIDGE

1921-1923   29

Who was the only vice president to be born on July 4th?

Calvin Coolidge was born July 4th, 1872.

Which three vice presidents died on July 4th?

Thomas Jefferson and John Adams in 1826 and Hannibal Hamlin in 1891.

Which two vice presidents died in office while serving the same president?

George Clinton died on April 20,1812 a year before the end of his and James Madison's first term. For the election of 1812, Madison was re-elected with Elbridge Gerry as his running mate. On November 23, 1814, Gerry died, leaving Madison once again without a vice president.

Which president and vice president, as a team, were the oldest to be inaugurated?

Harry Truman and Alben Barkley in 1948 were a combined 135 years old. Truman was 64 years old and Barkley was 71 years old on inauguration day.

Which president and vice president, as a team, were the youngest to be inaugurated?

Bill Clinton and Al Gore in 1992 were both a combined 90 years old. Clinton was 46 years old and Al Gore was 44 years old on inauguration day.

Which president and vice president, as a team, were the youngest to lose the election?

George McClellan and George Pendleton in 1864 were both a combined 76 years old. McClellan was 37 years old and Pendleton was 39 years old at the time of the election.

Which vice president suffered a stroke while addressing the U.S. Senate?

Henry Wilson suffered a stroke while addressing the U.S. Senate in 1875 and died shortly after that.

Which two vice presidents died on the same day?

Both Thomas Jefferson and John Adams died on the 50th anniversary of the signing of the Declaration of Independence, July 4th, 1826.

Who was the longest-lived vice president?

When John Nance Garner died on November 7, 1967, he was just 15 days short of his 99th birthday.

Who was the shortest-lived vice president?

Daniel Tompkins, who died at age 50, just three months after his term had expired.

How many vice presidents were older than the president they served?

22 vice presidents have been older than their president.

- George Clinton was four years older than Thomas Jefferson
- George Clinton was seven years older than James Madison
- Elbridge Gerry was seven years older than James Madison
- Richard Johnson was two years older than Martin Van Buren
- George Dallas was three years older than James Polk
- William King was eighteen years older than Franklin Pierce
- Andrew Johnson was three months older than Abraham Lincoln
- William Wheeler was three years older than Rutherford B. Hayes
- Chester Arthur was two years older than James Garfield
- Thomas Hendricks was eighteen years older than Grover Cleveland
- Levi Morton was nine years older than Benjamin Harrison
- Adlai Stevenson was two years older than Grover Cleveland
- Charles Fairbanks was six years older than Theodore Roosevelt

- James Sherman was two years older than William Howard Taft
- Thomas Marshall was two years older than Woodrow Wilson
- Charles Dawes was older than Calvin Coolidge
- Charles Curtis was fifteen years older than Herbert Hoover
- John Nance Garner was thirteen years older than Franklin Roosevelt
- Alben Barkley was seven years older than Harry Truman
- Lyndon Johnson was nine years older than John Kennedy
- Nelson Rockefeller was five years older than Gerald Ford
- Dick Cheney was two years older than George W. Bush

How many vice presidents were younger than the president they served?

25 vice presidents have been younger than their president.

- John Adams was younger than George Washington
- Thomas Jefferson was younger than John Adams
- Aaron Burr was younger than Thomas Jefferson
- Daniel Tompkins was younger than James Monroe
- John Calhoun was younger than John Quincy Adams
- John Calhoun was younger than Andrew Jackson
- Martin Van Buren was younger than Andrew Jackson
- John Tyler was younger than William Henry Harrison
- Millard Fillmore was younger than Zachary Taylor
- John Breckinridge was younger than James Buchanan
- Hannibal Hamlin was younger than Abraham Lincoln
- Schuyler Colfax was younger than Ulysses S. Grant
- Garret Hobart was younger than William McKinley
- Theodore Roosevelt was younger than William McKinley
- Calvin Coolidge was younger than Warren Harding
- Henry Wallace was younger than Franklin Roosevelt

- Harry Truman was younger than Franklin Roosevelt
- Richard Nixon was younger than Dwight Eisenhower
- Hubert Humphrey was younger than Lyndon Johnson
- Spiro Agnew was younger than Richard Nixon
- Gerald Ford was younger than Richard Nixon
- Walter Mondale was younger than Jimmy Carter
- George Bush was younger than Ronald Reagan
- Dan Quayle was younger than George Bush
- Al Gore was younger than Bill Clinton

What was the age of each vice president upon assuming office?

• John Adams.	53	
• Thomas Jefferson	53	
• Aaron Burr	45	
• George Clinton	65	under Jefferson
• George Clinton	69	under Madison
• Elbridge Gerry	68	
• Daniel Tompkins	42	
• John C. Calhoun	42	under John Quincy Adams
• John C. Calhoun	46	under Andrew Jackson
• Martin Van Buren	50	
• Richard Johnson	56	
• John Tyler	50	
• George Dallas	52	
• Millard Fillmore	49	
• William King	66	
• John Breckinridge	36	
• Hannibal Hamlin	51	
• Andrew Johnson	56	

- Schuyler Colfax   45
- Henry Wilson   61
- William Wheeler   57
- Chester Arthur   51
- Thomas Hendricks   65
- Levi Morton   64
- Adlai Stevenson   57
- Garret Hobart   52
- Theodore Roosevelt   42
- Charles Fairbanks   52
- James Sherman   53
- Thomas Marshall   58
- Calvin Coolidge   48
- Charles Dawes   59
- Charles Curtis   69
- John Nance Garner   64
- Henry Wallace   52
- Harry Truman   60
- Alben Barkley   71
- Richard Nixon   40
- Lyndon Baines Johnson   52
- Hubert Humphrey   53
- Spiro Agnew   51
- Gerald Ford   60
- Nelson Rockefeller   66
- Walter Mondale   49
- George Bush   56
- Dan Quayle   41
- Al Gore   44
- Dick Cheney   59

THEODORE ROOSEVELT

1901   25

How old was each vice president at the time of his death?

- John Adams.   90
- Thomas Jefferson   83
- Aaron Burr   80
- George Clinton   72
- Elbridge Gerry   70
- Daniel Tompkins   50
- John C. Calhoun   68
- Martin Van Buren   79
- Richard Johnson   70
- John Tyler   71
- George Dallas   72
- Millard Fillmore   74
- William King   67
- John Breckinridge   54
- Hannibal Hamlin   81
- Andrew Johnson   66
- Schuyler Colfax   61
- Henry Wilson   63
- William Wheeler   67
- Chester Arthur   57
- Thomas Hendricks   66
- Levi Morton   96
- Adlai Stevenson   78
- Garret Hobart   55
- Theodore Roosevelt   60
- Charles Fairbanks   66
- James Sherman   57

- Thomas Marshall   71
- Calvin Coolidge   60
- Charles Dawes   85
- Charles Curtis   76
- John Nance Garner   98
- Henry Wallace   77
- Harry Truman   88
- Alben Barkley   78
- Richard Nixon   81
- Lyndon Baines Johnson 65
- Hubert Humphrey   66
- Spiro Agnew   77
- Nelson Rockefeller   70

41

Just Passing Through

John Nance Garner was credited with saying the vice presidency was "not worth a warm bucket of spit."

During which American war were the most vice presidents, either past, present or future, alive?

During the four years that the United States was involved in the Civil War, 20 men who had been, were, or would be vice president, were alive at one time or another.

Who was the first vice president to be born after the Declaration of Independence in 1776?

Richard Johnson, who was born in 1780.

Who was the last vice president to be born in the 18th Century?

John Tyler, born in 1790.

Who was the last vice president to be born in the 19th Century?

Henry Wallace who was born in 1888.

At what three times have there been no living former vice presidents?

- Before John Adams assumed the Presidency in 1797, there had been no former vice presidents.

- With Hannibal Hamlin passing on July 4,1891, there were no living former vice presidents until Levi Morton left office on March 3,1993.

- After Levi Morton's death on May 16,1920, there were no living former vice presidents until March 3,1921, when Thomas Marshall left office.

How many future vice presidents were alive during the American Revolution?

There were 10 future vice presidents alive during America's Revolutionary War, including five who were active participants:

- John Adams
- Thomas Jefferson
- Aaron Burr
- George Clinton
- Elbridge Gerry
- Daniel Tompkins
- John Calhoun
- Martin Van Buren
- Richard Johnson
- William Rufus King

AARON BURR
1801~1805
3

How many past, present or future vice presidents were alive during the War of 1812?

There were 14 past, present and future vice presidents alive during the years of the War of 1812:

- John Adams
- Thomas Jefferson
- Aaron Burr
- Daniel Tompkins
- John Calhoun
- Martin Van Buren
- Richard Johnson
- John Tyler
- George Dallas
- Millard Fillmore
- William Rufus King

- Hannibal Hamlin
- Andrew Johnson
- Henry Wilson

How many past, present or future vice presidents were alive during the Mexican-American War?

There were 18 past, present and future vice presidents alive during the years of the Mexican-American War:

- John C. Calhoun
- Martin Van Buren
- Richard Johnson
- John Tyler
- George Dallas
- Millard Fillmore
- William King
- John Breckinridge
- Hannibal Hamlin
- Andrew Johnson
- Schuyler Colfax
- Henry Wilson
- William Wheeler
- Chester Arthur
- Thomas Hendricks
- Levi Morton
- Adlai Stevenson
- Garret Hobart

GARRET AUGUSTUS HOBART

1897-1899

24

How many past, present or future vice presidents were alive during the Civil War?

20 past, present and future vice presidents lived during the years of the Civil War:

- Martin Van Buren
- John Tyler
- George Dallas
- Millard Fillmore
- John Breckinridge
- Hannibal Hamlin
- Andrew Johnson
- Schuyler Colfax
- Henry Wilson
- William Wheeler
- Chester Arthur
- Thomas Hendricks
- Levi Morton
- Adlai Stevenson
- Garret Hobart
- Theodore Roosevelt
- Charles Fairbanks
- James Sherman
- Thomas Marshall
- Charles Curtis

How many past, present or future vice presidents were alive during World War One?

There were 16 past, present and future vice presidents alive during the years that America was involved in World War I:

- Theodore Roosevelt
- Charles Fairbanks
- Thomas Marshall
- Calvin Coolidge
- Charles G. Dawes
- Charles Curtis
- John Nance Garner
- Henry A. Wallace
- Harry S. Truman
- Alben W. Barkley
- Richard M. Nixon
- Lyndon B. Johnson
- Hubert H. Humphrey
- Spiro T. Agnew
- Gerald R. Ford
- Nelson Rockefeller

How many past, present or future vice presidents were alive during World War Two?

14 past, present and future vice presidents lived during the years that America was involved in World War II:

- Charles G. Dawes
- John Nance Garner
- Henry A. Wallace
- Harry S. Truman
- Alben W. Barkley
- Richard M. Nixon

- Lyndon B. Johnson
- Hubert H. Humphrey
- Spiro T. Agnew
- Gerald R. Ford
- Nelson Rockefeller
- Walter Mondale
- George Bush
- Dick Cheney

How many past, present or future vice presidents were alive during the Korean War?

There were 16 past, present and future vice presidents alive during the years of the Korean War:

- Charles G. Dawes
- John Nance Garner
- Henry A. Wallace
- Harry S. Truman
- Alben W. Barkley
- Richard M. Nixon
- Lyndon B. Johnson
- Hubert H. Humphrey
- Spiro T. Agnew
- Gerald R. Ford
- Nelson Rockefeller
- Walter Mondale
- George Bush
- Dan Quayle
- Al Gore
- Dick Cheney

How many past, present or future vice presidents were alive during the Vietnam War?

There were 14 past, present and future vice presidents alive during the years of the Vietnam War:

- John Nance Garner
- Henry A. Wallace
- Harry S. Truman
- Richard M. Nixon
- Lyndon B. Johnson
- Hubert H. Humphrey
- Spiro T. Agnew
- Gerald R. Ford
- Nelson Rockefeller
- Walter Mondale
- George Bush
- Dan Quayle
- Al Gore
- Dick Cheney

How many past, present or future vice presidents were alive during the Persian Gulf War?

There were eight past, present and future vice presidents alive during the Persian Gulf War:

- Richard M. Nixon
- Spiro T. Agnew
- Gerald R. Ford
- Walter Mondale
- George Bush
- Dan Quayle
- Al Gore
- Dick Cheney

How many past and present vice presidents were alive during the War on Terrorism?

There are currently six former or current vice presidents alive during the War on Terrorism:

- Gerald R. Ford
- Walter Mondale
- George Bush
- Dan Quayle
- Al Gore
- Dick Cheney

How many vice presidents were alive on January 1, 2004?

There were six vice presidents alive on that date:

- Dick Cheney
- Al Gore
- Dan Quayle
- George Bush
- Walter Mondale
- Gerald Ford

In what specific year were the most past, present or future vice presidents alive at the same time?

In 1824 and 1868 there were 19 past, present or future vice presidents living. From 1864 until 1865 there were 18 living.

1824

- John Adams   past
- Thomas Jefferson   past
- Aaron Burr   past

- Daniel Tompkins   present
- Richard Johnson   future
- John Calhoun   future
- Martin Van Buren   future
- William King   future
- John Tyler   future
- George Dallas   future
- Millard Fillmore   future
- Andrew Johnson   future
- Hannibal Hamlin   future
- Henry Wilson   future
- William Wheeler   future
- Thomas Hendricks   future
- John Breckinridge   future
- Schuyler Colfax   future
- Levi Morton   future

8

1868

- Millard Fillmore   past
- Andrew Johnson   past
- Hannibal Hamlin   past
- Henry Wilson   future
- William Wheeler   future
- Thomas Hendricks   future
- John Breckinridge   future
- Schuyler Colfax   future
- Levi Morton   future
- Chester Arthur   future
- Adlai Stevenson   future
- Garret Hobart   future
- Charles Fairbanks   future
- Thomas Marshall   future

- James Sherman   future
- Theodore Roosevelt   future
- Charles Curtis   future
- Charles Dawes   future
- John Nance Garner   future

1864

- George Dallas   past
- Millard Fillmore   past
- Andrew Johnson   past
- Hannibal Hamlin   present
- Henry Wilson   future
- William Wheeler   future
- Thomas Hendricks   future
- John Breckinridge   future
- Schuyler Colfax   future
- Levi Morton   future
- Chester Arthur   future
- Adlai Stevenson   future
- Garret Hobart   future
- Charles Fairbanks   future
- Thomas Marshall   future
- James Sherman   future
- Theodore Roosevelt   future
- Charles Curtis   future

1865

- Millard Fillmore   past
- Hannibal Hamlin   past
- Andrew Johnson   present
- Henry Wilson   future
- William Wheeler   future
- Thomas Hendricks   future

- John Breckinridge   future
- Schuyler Colfax   future
- Levi Morton   future
- Chester Arthur   future
- Adlai Stevenson   future
- Garret Hobart   future
- Charles Fairbanks   future
- Thomas Marshall   future
- James Sherman   future
- Theodore Roosevelt   future
- Charles Curtis   future
- Charles Dawes   future

Which vice presidents were in office during wartime?

- George Dallas   Mexican American War
- Hannibal Hamlin   Civil War
- Andrew Johnson   Civil War
- Garret Hobart   Spanish American War
- Thomas Marshall   World War One
- Henry Wallace   World War Two
- Harry Truman   World War Two
- Alben Barkley   Korean War
- Richard Nixon   Vietnam War
- Lyndon Johnson   Vietnam War
- Hubert Humphrey   Vietnam War
- Spiro Agnew   Vietnam War
- Gerald Ford   Vietnam War
- Nelson Rockefeller   Vietnam War

Getting In And Out
Of The Office

Henry Wilson was an expert cobbler before becoming Vice President.

Which vice president ran unopposed?

In 1820, Daniel Tompkins ran unopposed, the only time there has been no losing vice presidential candidate. The Federalist party folded prior to the general election and provided no opponents for President James Monroe and Daniel Tompkins.

Who was the vice president of the Confederate States of America?

Alexander Stephens held that post from 1861 until the end of the war in 1865.

Who was the first vice president to be sworn in by a female justice?

Al Gore.

Which vice president along with his presidential running mate lost both the popular vote and electoral vote yet still won the election?

In the election of 1876, Rutherford B. Hayes and William Wheeler lost both the popular vote and the electoral vote, however the ticket of Samuel Tilden and Thomas Hendricks fell one electoral vote shy of the 185 total needed be declared the winner, after republicans challenged the returns of four states. In exchange for the removal of federal troops from Southern states, the disputed Southern states electoral votes were given to Hayes and the election was certified just 3 days before the inauguration.

Which two vice presidents served under two presidents?

- George Clinton was Thomas Jefferson's second vice president. Clinton also ran for vice president with James Madison in a successful bid.

- John C. Calhoun was not renominated by John Quincy Adams in 1828. Instead, Calhoun ran with Andrew Jackson and was victorious, thereby serving his two terms with two different presidents.

Who is the only vice president to be sworn into office outside of the United States?

In the 1852 election Franklin Pierce and William King won, but King was ill and traveled to Cuba. A special act of Congress allowed him to take his oath in Havana, Cuba.

Who is the only vice president ever elected by the Senate?

In 1836, Martin Van Buren and Richard Johnson won the popular election, but Johnson was left one electoral vote short of the majority needed to win when some electors did not vote for him. He then won election in the Senate, 33-16.

After William McKinley was assassinated, where did Theodore Roosevelt take the oath of office?

Theodore Roosevelt was inaugurated President following the death of William McKinley in the Wilcox Mansion, located in Buffalo, New York. The Mansion is now known as the Theodore Roosevelt Inaugural National Historic Site.

What vice president, upon death of the President, was sworn into office by his father?

Calvin Coolidge was in Vermont visiting his father when he was informed of the death of Warren Harding. His father, a notary public and magistrate administered the Oath of Office to the new President.

Which two vice presidents are the only ones to run together and win election as President and Vice President?

Richard Nixon and Spiro Agnew. Nixon had served under President Eisenhower and Agnew was Nixon's Vice President, when they won re-election in 1972.

Which vice president served as president and never had their own vice president?

- John Tyler   1841-1845
- Millard Fillmore   1850-1853
- Andrew Johnson   1865-1869
- Chester Arthur   1881-1885

Which vice president served as president and did not have a vice president until winning election on their own?

- Theodore Roosevelt   1901-1905
- Calvin Coolidge   1923-1925
- Harry Truman   1945-1949
- Lyndon Johnson   1963-1965

More Than Just A Pretty Face

Gerald Ford was once a professional model.

Which vice presidents won the Noble Prize?

Theodore Roosevelt won the Noble peace prize in 1905, while president, for developing the treaty that ended the war between Russia and Japan.

The 1925 Noble Prize was awarded to Vice President Charles Dawes, for the creation of the Dawes Plan, a program to restore the German economy after World War One.

Which vice president prepared a Manual of Parliamentary Practice for the United States Senate, which though unofficial, has served as a resource for Senators ever since?

Thomas Jefferson wrote the manual while serving as Vice President.

Which vice president wrote a multi-volume history of the United States?

Henry Wilson wrote a multi-volume history of the United States, the first two volumes published in 1872 and 1874, with the third volume appearing in 1876, after his death.

What vice president wrote the song "It's All In The Game"?

Charles Dawes.

128

Which vice president was credited with killing Tecumseh, the great Indian war chief, in the war of 1812?

Richard Johnson was a colonel serving under General William Henry Harrison when they came across 800 British troops and 1,200 Indians. Harrison led the U.S. troops to victory while Johnson led the charge in which Tecumseh was killed.

Which vice president shot and killed the Secretary of the Treasury?

Aaron Burr killed Alexander Hamilton in 1804. Burr had a long running feud with Alexander Hamilton that culminated in a duel in Weehawken, New Jersey. Burr was indicted for murder in both New Jersey and New York, though was never brought to trial. Burr had become Vice President by coming in second to Thomas Jefferson in 1800, but was replaced by George Clinton as the nominee in 1804, thereby becoming the last vice president elected in that manner.

Which vice president is credited with coining the term "senators"?

John Calhoun came up with the term "senators". Until then, they had been referred to as Gentlemen of Congress.

Which vice president was responsible for creating the system of gerrymandering, the redistricting of precincts for political advantage?

Elbridge Gerry.

What former vice president left the Union and joined the Confederate army to serve as a General?

John Breckinridge served from 1857-1861 under President Buchanan. After leaving office, he became one of the Senators from Kentucky, and then shortly after that, left the Senate to join the Confederate army.

Which vice president enlisted for guard duty during his term in office?

After the outbreak of the Civil War, Hannibal Hamlin returned to his home in Maine and joined the Maine Coast Guard, where he was made a cook and never rose above the rank of private.

Which vice president, as a member of the Senate had openly opposed the 13th, 14th and 15th Amendments?

As a member of the Senate Thomas Hendricks openly opposed the amendments that dealt with freedom for slaves, voting rights and citizenship.

What vice president had made a fortune by putting guns on his company's fishing vessels and renting them to the U.S. government as war ships?

Elbridge Gerry, during the Revolutionary War.

Who was the richest vice president?

Nelson Rockefeller, whose grandfather founded Standard Oil, had a net worth of over $1 billion in the mid-1970s. Dan Quayle, whose family made a fortune in newspapers, was also reported to have family assets of close to $1 billion.

Which vice president had proposed requiring postal employees to work seven days a week because he enjoyed receiving mail?

As a Congressman, Richard Johnson suggested the seven-day workweek for postal employees, but the idea was rejected.

Which vice president took up golf because the president had taken it up?

When William Howard Taft took up golf, James Sherman did the same so that he could accompany the President on his outings, however, Sherman was such a poor player President Taft stopped inviting him to join his foursome.

Which vice president regularly spent Sunday evenings at the White House, drinking lemonade and singing hymns around the piano?

William Wheeler was a regular guest at the Rutherford B. Hayes White House where Mrs. Hayes had banned alcohol, dancing, profanity, any music besides hymns, and any other activity deemed to be a vice.

Which vice president spent his own money to have the Seal of the Vice Presidency redesigned?

Nelson Rockefeller in 1975.

Which vice president had been a male model?

In his late 20s, Gerald Ford was convinced to give modeling a try and he appeared in Look Magazine and on the cover of Cosmopolitan.

If Only They
Called Me Mr. Tibbs

Thomas Marshall enjoyed his cigars as Vice President from 1913-1921.

Which vice president was referred to as "His Royal Rotundy"?

By trying to attend most Senate meetings and debates, John Adams irritated many Senators who called him "His Royal Rotundy" or "His Mighty Benign Highness."

Which vice president was known as "Smiler"?

Schuyler Colfax of Indiana. Colfax was known as friendly and amiable with a constant grin as speaker of the house for six years.

Which vice president was known as the "Farmers Boy"?

Daniel Tompkins.

Which vice president did President Andrew Jackson refer to as Miss Nancy?

William King.

Which vice president was nicknamed "Cactus Jack"?

John Nance Garner.

Why was Charles Dawes known as "Hell and Maria"?

During a congressional inquiry, Dawes was heard to have said "Helen Maria, I'd have paid horse prices for sheep if the sheep could have pulled artillery to the front!"

Which vice president was known as the "Cobbler of Natick "?

Henry Wilson who had served as an apprentice shoemaker and owned a shoe factory.

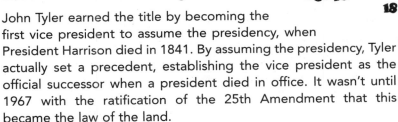

Which vice president was known as "His Accidency"?

John Tyler earned the title by becoming the first vice president to assume the presidency, when President Harrison died in 1841. By assuming the presidency, Tyler actually set a precedent, establishing the vice president as the official successor when a president died in office. It wasn't until 1967 with the ratification of the 25th Amendment that this became the law of the land.

What vice president was born Leslie King?

Gerald Ford.

What vice president was born Jeremiah Jones Colbath?

Henry Wilson.

Which vice president was known as the "Little Magician"?

Martin Van Buren.

Love, Marriage And
The Repercussions

*Spiro Agnew, Gerald Ford and Nelson Rockefeller shared
the vice presidency from 1973-1977.*

Who was the only bachelor to serve as vice president?

William King?

Who was the first vice president to marry in office?

On November 18, 1949, in St. Louis, Missouri, 71 year old Alben Barkley, married Elizabeth Jane Rucker Hadley, his 38-year-old sweetheart.

Which two vice presidents were married on their birthdays?

- John Tyler married Letitia Christian on his twenty-third birthday, which was March 29, 1813.

- Theodore Roosevelt married Alice Lee on his twenty-second birthday, October 22, 1880.

Which vice president fathered the most children?

John Tyler with 15.

How old was John Tyler when his wife gave birth to their last child?

He was 70 years old.

Which vice president named his children after George and Martha Washington?

George Clinton had a fond relationship with George and Martha Washington and named his children George Washington Clinton and Martha Washington Clinton.

Which vice president had a grandson run for president?

Adlai Ewing Stevenson's grandson, also named Adlai Ewing Stevenson ran for president twice, losing in both 1952 and 1956 to Dwight Eisenhower.

Which vice president's cousin ran for vice president?

Theodore Roosevelt's cousin was Franklin Roosevelt. He ran unsuccessfully for vice president in 1920.

Besides being president, Governor of New York, and Assistant Secretary of the Navy, what other political experience did cousins Theodore Roosevelt and Franklin Roosevelt have in common?

They both ran for vice president, Theodore Roosevelt successfully in 1900 and Franklin Roosevelt unsuccessfully in 1920.

What vice president's divorce was finalized on the day he died?

Aaron Burr died on his eightieth birthday, the same day his second wife's divorce was finalized on the grounds of his adultery.

They Said It,
They Really Said It

*Richard Johnson loved mail —
he tried to have it delivered seven days a week.*

Which vice president said: *"Once there were two brothers. One ran away to sea; the other was elected vice president of the United States. And nothing was heard of either of them again."*?

Thomas Marshall.

Which vice president believed that the presidency should be for life and that members of Congress should be granted seats on a hereditary system?

John Adams.

What former vice president upon his retirement turned down an honorary degree from Oxford University by saying that he did nothing to deserve it and that no one knew who he was?

Millard Fillmore, who actually made the claim after having been President.

Which vice president admitted that he might have been one of the worst Presidents of the Senate ever?

Theodore Roosevelt, who admitted to sleeping through sessions and enrolled in law school while Vice President because of boredom.

What message did Vice President Thomas Marshall telegraph to Calvin Coolidge upon his election as vice president in 1920?

Marshall's message to Coolidge was "Please accept my sincere sympathies."

SPIRO THEODORE AGNEW

1969-1973

39

Which vice president said: *"Some newspapers dispose of their garbage by printing it."*?

Spiro Agnew.

Which vice president said, *"One useless man is a disgrace, two a law firm, three or more a Congress."*?

John Adams.

What Vice President defined the office perfectly when he said: *"I am not in a leadership position. I am supporting the President. He can exert the leadership and I can support him."*?

Nelson Rockefeller.

What was Rutherford Hayes response when informed that William Wheeler had been nominated to be his vice presidential candidate?

Upon hearing the news, Hayes politely asked, "Who is Wheeler?"

Who claimed that the vice presidency was *"not worth a warm bucket of spit."*?

John Nance Garner.

What vice president coined the phrase, *"What this country needs is a really good five cent cigar."*?

Thomas Marshall.

Why did Calvin Coolidge say he enjoyed his time as vice president?

Coolidge claimed that the job never interfered with his mandatory eleven hours of sleep a day.

Who claimed that taking the job of vice president was *"the worst damn fool mistake I ever made."*?

John Nance Garner.

Which vice president said he didn't campaign in inner cities, because, *"If you've seen one slum you've seen them all."*?

Spiro Agnew.

Which vice president defined the vice presidency by saying: *"The Vice Presidency is the most insignificant office that ever the invention of man contrived or his imagination conceived."*?

John Adams.

Which vice president was said by his wife to enjoy golf more than sex?

To dispel rumors of infidelity by her husband with a female admirer on the golf course, Marilyn Quayle said of the Vice President, "Everyone knows Dan would rather play golf than have sex any day".

44

Which president once said, in response to a reporters question about a major policy contributed by then vice president Richard Nixon: *"If you give me a week, I might think of one."*?

Dwight Eisenhower.

Which vice president said: *"A little over a week ago, I took a rather unusual step for a vice president...I said something."*?

Spiro Agnew.

What Vice President stated that *"The second office of this government is honorable and easy, the first is but a splendid misery."*?

Thomas Jefferson.

"Look at all the Vice Presidents in history. Where are they? They were about as useful as a cow's fifth teat."

Harry S. Truman.

"I would a great deal rather be anything, say professor of history, than vice president."

Theodore Roosevelt.

"This is a hell of a job. I can only do two things: one is to sit up here and listen to you birds talk....The other is to look at newspapers every morning to see how the president's health is."

Charles Dawes, speaking to Alben Barkley.

"Genius enough to have made him immortal, and unschooled passion enough to have made him infamous".

Woodrow Wilson, commenting about Aaron Burr.

"If the tide of defamation and abuse shall turn and my administration come to be praised, future vice presidents who may succeed to the presidency may feel some slight encouragement to pursue an independent course."

John Tyler.

"I should hate to think that the Senate was as tired of me at the beginning of my service as I am of the Senate at the end."

Charles G. Dawes.

"Keep your mouth shut, your head down, and don't act like you want it."

Jack Kemp, discussing the vice presidency.

"Vice president — it has such a nice ring to it!"

Geraldine Ferraro, 1984.

"Senator, I served with Jack Kennedy, I knew Jack Kennedy, Jack Kennedy was a friend of mine. Senator, you are no Jack Kennedy."

Lloyd Bentsen, to Dan Quayle, in 1988 Vice Presidential Debate.

"I do not propose to be buried until I am really dead."

Daniel Webster, on not accepting the Vice Presidency.

"The President has only 190 million bosses. The Vice President has 190 million and one."

Hubert Humphrey.

"This man is certainly deranged."

Attorney General James Speed's remarks during Andrew Johnson's vice presidential acceptance address in 1865.

Stuff That Doesn't Fit Anywhere Else

Hannibal Hamlin served as a cook in the navy during his term as Vice President.

Who was the shortest Vice President?

Martin Van Buren who stood five feet, six inches tall was the shortest vice president.

Who was the tallest vice president?

At six feet, three inches, Lyndon Johnson was the tallest vice president.

How could the vice president be born in a different country than the United States if the constitution mandates the vice president be born in the United States?

Prior to the development of the United States, the framers were from several different countries, including England, the country America seceded from. While they were born in what was to be the United States, they were actually English citizens at birth.

Which vice president is rumored to have been born outside the United States and therefore ineligible for the office?

The birthplace of Chester Arthur is listed as Fairfield, Vermont, near the Canadian border. It was rumored that he was born on the Canadian side.

Who was the last vice president to be born in a log cabin?

Alben Barkley who was born in 1877.

Which vice president attended the constitutional convention but refused to sign the Constitution because, in his view, it didn't provide states with enough rights?

Elbridge Gerry, the nations fifth vice president.

Which former vice presidents supported the Confederate States in the Civil War?

- John Breckinridge served as a General for the Confederacy in the Civil War.

- John Tyler was elected to the House of Representatives of the Confederate Congress, but passed away in 1862 before the Confederate Congress had assembled. He was the only former United States President to serve for the Confederacy.

Which two vice presidents served in two different centuries?

Thomas Jefferson served from 1797 until 1801 and Al Gore held the office from 1993 until 2001.

Why are William Wheeler and Thomas Hendricks intertwined in history?

45

Wheeler, running with Rutherford Hayes won the election though Samuel Tilden and Hendricks had more votes. Eight years later Hendricks was elected Vice President on a ticket with Grover Cleveland.

What does the eighth vice president have in common with the eighth president, and what does the tenth vice president have in common with the tenth president?

They were the same person.

- Martin Van Buren was the eighth vice president, and was elected to become the eighth president.

- John Tyler was the tenth vice president, and ascended to the Presidency as the tenth president when William Henry Harrison died.

What vice president owned a house referred to as the Little Cream White House?

Because of its excess lavishness, Garret Hobart's Vice Presidential residence was referred to as the Little Cream White House.

What vice president misspelled the word "Potato" in front of a class of school aged children?

Dan Quayle.

Who was vice president when the Constitution celebrated its fiftieth anniversary?

Richard Johnson.

Who served as vice president, and president of the Senate, when Senator Henry Foote drew a pistol on Senator Thomas Hart Benton in the Senate chambers?

Millard Fillmore.

Since 1976 there has been a Bush or a Dole on every Republican ticket. How is this possible?

- 1976 Bob Dole Vice Presidential Nominee
- 1980 George Bush Vice Presidential Nominee
- 1984 George Bush Vice Presidential Nominee
- 1988 George Bush Presidential Nominee
- 1992 George Bush Presidential Nominee
- 1996 Bob Dole Presidential Nominee
- 2000 George W. Bush Presidential Nominee
- 2004 George W. Bush Presidential Nominee

Who were the two candidates for Vice President in 1984?

Geraldine Ferraro and George Bush.

Who was Abraham Lincoln's first vice president?

Hannibal Hamlin.

HANNIBAL HAMLIN

1861-1865

15

Hubert Horatio Humphrey was nominated as vice president in what year?

1964.

What did Hale E. Dougherty have to do with Spiro Agnew?

Hale E. Dougherty co-created the Spiro Agnew watch in the early 1970's. The watch became a national fashion statement as it lampooned Richard Nixon's first Vice President.

Who was Alexander Throttlebottom?

He was the bumbling Vice President of the United States and a fictitious character, in the 1931 play "Of Thee I Sing," by Ira and George Gershwin and George S. Kaufman. The character was supposedly based on then Vice President Charles Curtis.

What was the name of the first vice president to serve on the television program "The West Wing" and who portrayed him?

The character was John Hoynes, played by Tim Matheson.

What was the name of the second vice president to serve on the television program "The West Wing" and who portrayed him?

The character was Robert Russell, played by Gary Cole.

Appendix

William King, ill and dying, was the only Vice President to take the Vice Presidential oath in Cuba.

Vice Presidents Of The United States

Date and Place of Birth and
Date and Place of Death

Adams, John	19 Oct 1735 Braintree, MA	4 Jul 1826 Quincy, MA
Jefferson, Thomas	2 Apr 1743 Shadwell, VA	4 Jul 1826 Charlottesville, VA
Burr, Aaron	6 Feb 1756 Newark, NJ	14 Sep 1836 Staten Island, NY
Clinton, George	26 Jul 1739 Little Britain, NY	20 Apr 1812 Washington, DC
Gerry, Elbridge	17 Jul 1744 Marblehead, MA	23 Nov 1814 Washington, DC
Tompkins, Daniel	21 Jun 1774 Fox Meadow, NY	11 Jun 1825 Tompkinsville, NY
Calhoun, John	18 Mar 1782 Abbeville Dist., SC	31 Mar 1850 Washington, DC
Van Buren, Martin	5 Dec 1782 Kinderhook, NY	24 Jul 1862 Kinderhook, NY
Johnson, Richard Mentor	17 Oct 1780 Bryant's Station, KY	19 Nov 1850 Frankfort, KY
Tylyer, John	29 Mar 1790 Charles City co., VA	18 Jan 1862 Richmond, VA
Dallas, George Mifflin	10 Jul 1792 Philadelphia, PA	31 Dec 1864 Philadelphia, PA
Fillmore, Millard	7 Jan 1800 Summerhill, NY	8 Mar 1874 Buffalo, NY
King, William Rufus Devane	7 Apr 1786 Sampson co., NC	18 Apr 1853 Cahaba, AL
Breckinridge, John Cabell	16 Jan 1821 Lexington, KY	17 May 1875 Lexington, KY

Hamlin, Hannibal	27 Aug 1809 Paris, ME	4 Jul 1891 Bangor, ME
Johnson, Andrew	29 Dec 1808 Raleigh, NC	31 Jul 1875 Carter's Station, TN
Colfax, Schuyler	23 Mar 1823 New York City, NY	13 Jan 1885 Mankato, MN
Wilson, Henry	16 Feb 1812 Farmington, NH	22 Nov 1875 Washington, DC
Wheeler, William Almon	30 Jun 1819 Malone, NY	4 Jun 1887 Malone, NY
Arthur, Chester Alan	5 Oct 1829 Fairfield, VT	18 Nov 1886 New York City, NY
Hendricks, Thomas Andrews	7 Sep 1819 Muskingham co., OH	25 Nov 1885 Indianapolis, IN
Morton, Levi Parsons	16 May 1824 Shoreham, VT	16 May 1920 Rhinebeck, NY
Stevenson, Adlia Ewing	23 Oct 1835 Christian co., KY	14 Jun 1914 Chicago, IL
Hobart, Garret Augustus	3 Jun 1844 Long Branch, NJ	21 Nov 1899 Paterson, NJ
Roosevelt, Theodore	27 Oct 1858 New York City, NY	6 Jan 1919 Oyster Bay, NY
Fairbanks, Charles Warren	11 May 1852 Union county, OH	4 Jun 1918 Indianapolis, IN
Sherman, James Schoolcraft	24 Oct 1855 Utica, NY	30 Oct 1912 Utica, NY
Marshall, Thomas Riley	14 Mar 1854 North Manchester, IN	1 Jun 1925 Washington, DC
Coolidge, John Calvin	4 Jul 1872 Plymouth, VT	5 Jan 1933 Northampton, MA
Dawes, Charles Gates	27 Aug 1865 Marietta, GA	23 Apr 1951 Evanson, IL

Curtis, Charles	25 Jan 1860 Topeka, KS	8 Feb 1936 Washington, DC
Garner, John Nance	22 Nov 1868 Detroit, TX	7 Nov 1967 Uvalde, TX
Wallace, Henry Agard	7 Oct 1888 Orient, IA	18 Nov 1965 Danbury, CT
Truman, Harry S.	8 May 1884 Lamar, MO	26 Dec 1972 Kansas City, MO
Barkley, Alben William	24 Nov 1877 Lowes, KY	30 Apr 1956 Lexington, VA
Nixon, Richard Milhous	9 Jan 1913 Yorba Linda, CA	22 Apr 1994 New York City, NY
Johnson, Lyndon Baines	27 Aug 1908 Stonewall, TX	22 Jan 1973 San Antonio, TX
Humphrey, Hubert Horatio, Jr.	27 May 1911 Wallace, SD	13 Jan 1978 Waverly, MN
Agnew, Spiro Theodore	9 Nov 1918 Baltimore, MD	17 Sep 1996 Berlin, MD
Ford, Gerald Rudolph	14 Jul 1914 Omaha, NE	Living
Rockefeller, Nelson Aldrich	8 Jul 1908 Bar Harbor, ME	26 Jan 1979 New York City, NY
Mondale, Walter Frederick	5 Jan 1928 Ceylon, MN	Living
Bush, George Herbert Walker	12 Jun 1924 Milton, MA	Living
Quayle, James Danforth	4 Feb 1947 Indianapolis, IN	Living
Gore, Albert Arnold, Jr.	31 Mar 1948 Washington, DC	Living
Cheney, Richard Bruce	30 Jan 1941 Lincoln, NE	Living

Vice Presidents And Their Birthdates By Month

Walter Mondale, **5th,** 1928	Millard Fillmore, **7th,** 1800	Richard Nixon, **9th,** 1913	John Breckinridge, **16th,** 1821	Charles Curtis, **25th,** 1860	Dick Cheney, **30th,** 1941	
Dan Quayle, **4th,** 1947	Aaron Burr, **6th,** 1756	Henry Wilson, **16th,** 1812				
Thomas Marshall, **14th,** 1854	John Calhoun, **18th,** 1782	Schuyler Colfax, **23rd,** 1823	John Tyler **29th,** 1790	Al Gore, **31st,** 1948		
William King, **7th,** 1786	Thomas Jefferson, **13th,** 1743					
Harry Truman, **8th,** 1884	Charles Fairbanks, **11th,** 1852	Levi Morton, **16th,** 1824	Hubert Humphrey, **27th,** 1911			
Garrett Hobart, **3rd,** 1844	George Bush, **12th,** 1924	Daniel Thompkins, **21st,** 1774	William Wheeler, **30th,** 1819			
Calvin Coolidge, **4th,** 1872	Nelson Rockefeller, **8th,** 1908	George Dallas, **10th,** 1792	Gerald Ford **14th,** 1913	Elbridge Gerry, **17th,** 1744	George Clinton, **26th,** 1739	
Hannibal Hamlin, **27th,** 1809	Charles Dawes, **27th,** 1865	Lyndon Johnson **27th,** 1908				
Thomas Hendricks, **7th,** 1819						
Chester Arthur, **5th,** 1929	Henry Wallace, **7th,** 1888	Richard Johnson, **17th,** 1780	John Adams, **19th,** 1735	Adlai Stevenson, **23rd,** 1835	James Sherman, **24th,** 1855	Theodore Roosevelt, **27th,** 1858
Spiro Agnew, **9th,** 1918	John Nance Garner, **22nd,** 1868	Alben Barkley, **24th,** 1877				
Martin Van Buren, **6th,** 1782	Andrew Johnson, **29th,** 1808					

Vice Presidents And Their Wives

(Maiden Names)

John Adams and Abigail Smith

Thomas Jefferson and Martha (Wayles) Skelton

Aaron Burr and Theodosia (Bartow) Prevost

Aaron Burr and Eliza (Bowen) Jumel

George Clinton and Cornelia Tappen

Elbridge Gerry and Ann Thompson

Daniel Tompkins and Hannah Minthorne

John Calhoun and Floride Bonneau

Martin Van Buren and Hannah Hoes

Richard Johnson and Julia Chinn**

John Tyler and Letitia Christian

John Tyler and Julia Gardiner

George Dallas and Sophia Chew Nicklin

Millard Fillmore and Abigail Powers

Millard Fillmore and Caroline Carmichael McIntosh

William King – Unmarried

John Breckinridge and Mary Cyrene Burch

Hannibal Hamlin and Sarah Jane Emery

Hannibal Hamlin and Ellen Vesta Emery

Andrew Johnson and Eliza McCardle

Schuyler Colfax and Evelyn E. Clark

Schuyler Colfax and Ellen Maria Wade

Henry Wilson and Harriet Malvina Howe

William Wheeler and Mary King

Chester Arthur and Ellen Lewis Herndon

Thomas Hendricks and Eliza C. Morgan

Levi Morton and Lucy Young Kimball

Levi Morton and Anna Livingston

Adlai Stevenson and Letitia Green

Garret Hobart and Esther Jane Tuttle

Theodore Roosevelt and Alice Hathaway Lee

Theodore Roosevelt and Edith Kermit Carow

Charles Fairbanks and Cornelia Cole

James Sherman and Carrie Babcock

Thomas Marshall and Lois Irene Kimsey

Calvin Coolidge and Grace Anna Goodhue

Charles Dawes and Caro Dana Blymyer

Charles Curtis and Anna Elizabeth Baird

John Nance Garner and Marietta Elizabeth Rheiner

Henry Wallace and Ilo Browne

Harry Truman and Elizabeth Virginia Wallace

Alben Barkley and Dorothy Anne Brower

Alben Barkley and Elizabeth Jane (Rucker) Hadley

Richard Nixon and Thelma Catherine (Pat) Ryan

Lyndon Johnson and Claudia Alta Taylor

Hubert Humphrey and Muriel Fay Buck

Spiro Agnew and Elinor Isabel Judefind

Gerald Ford and Elizabeth Anne (Bloomer) Warren

Nelson Rockefeller and Mary Todhunter Clark

Nelson Rockefeller and Margaretta Large (Fitler) Murphy

Walter Mondale and Joan Adams

George Bush and Barbara Pierce

Dan Quayle and Marilyn Tucker

Al Gore and Mary Elizabeth Aitcheson

Dick Cheney and Lynne Vincent

**Common Law Marriage

First Name's Of Vice Presidents

Aaron   (Burr)
Adlai   (Stevenson)
Al   (Gore)
Alben   (Barkley)
Calvin   (Coolidge)
Charles   (Fairbanks, Dawes, Curtis)
Chester   (Arthur)
Daniel   (Thompkins, Quayle)
Elbridge   (Gerry)
Garret   (Hobart)
George   (Clinton, Dallas, Bush)
Gerald   (Ford)
Hannibal   (Hamlin)
Harry   (Truman)
Henry   (Wilson, Wallace)
Hubert   (Humphrey)
James   (Sherman)
John   (Adams, Calhoun, Tyler, Breckinridge, Garner)
Levi   (Morton)
Lyndon   (Johnson)
Martin   (Van Buren)
Millard   (Fillmore)
Nelson   (Rockefeller)
Richard   (Johnson, Nixon, Cheney)
Schuyler   (Colfax)
Spiro   (Agnew)
Theodore   (Roosevelt)
Thomas   (Jefferson, Hendricks, Marshall)
Walter   (Mondale)
William   (King, Wheeler)

Last Name's Of Vice Presidents

Adams	(John)
Agnew	(Spiro)
Arthur	(Chester)
Barkley	(Alben)
Breckinridge	(John)
Burr	(Aaron)
Bush	(George)
Calhoun	(John)
Cheney	(Dick)
Clinton	(George)
Colfax	(Schuyler)
Coolidge	(Calvin)
Curtis	(Charles)
Dallas	(George)
Dawes	(Charles)
Fairbanks	(Charles)
Fillmore	(Millard)
Ford	(Gerald)
Garner	(John)
Gerry	(Elbridge)
Gore	(Al)
Hamlin	(Hannibal)
Henricks	(Thomas)
Hobart	(Garret)
Humphrey	(Hubert)
Jefferson	(Thomas)
Johnson	(Richard, Andrew, Lyndon)
King	(William)
Marshall	(Thomas)

Mondale	(Walter)
Morton	(Levi)
Nixon	(Richard)
Quayle	(Dan)
Rockefeller	(Nelson)
Roosevelt	(Theodore)
Sherman	(James)
Stevenson	(Adlai)
Tompkins	(Daniel)
Truman	(Harry)
Tyler	(John)
Van Buren	(Martin)
Wallace	(Henry)
Wheeler	(William)
Wilson	(Henry)

1865   16

That Was Fun, Now What?

What did each vice president do after leaving office?

John Adams	President
Thomas Jefferson	President
Aaron Burr	Private Citizen
George Clinton	Died in Office
Elbridge Gerry	Died in Office
Daniel Tompkins	Private Citizen
John Calhoun	U.S. Senate
Martin Van Buren	President
Richard Johnson	Private Citizen
John Tyler	President
George Dallas	Private Citizen
Millard Fillmore	President
William King	Died in Office
John Breckinridge	Private Citizen
Hannibal Hamlin	U.S. Senate
Andrew Johnson	President
Schyler Colfax	Private Citizen
Henry Wilson	Died in Office
William Wheeler	Private Citizen
Chester Arthur	President
Thomas Hendricks	Died in Office
Levi Morton	Private Citizen
Adlai Stevenson	Private Citizen
Garret Hobart	Died in Office
Theodore Roosevelt	President
Charles Fairbanks	Private Citizen

James Sherman	Died in Office
Thomas Marshall	Private Citizen
Calvin Coolidge	President
Charles Dawes	Private Citizen
Charles Cutis	Private Citizen
John Nance Garner	Private Citizen
Henry Wallace	Private Citizen
Harry Truman	President
Alben Barkley	Private Citizen
Richard Nixon	Private Citizen / President
Lyndon Johnson	President
Hubert Humphrey	U.S. Senator
Spiro Agnew	Private Citizen
Gerald Ford	President
Nelson Rockefeller	Private Citizen
Walter Mondale	Private Citizen
George Bush	President
Dan Quayle	Private Citizen
Al Gore	Private Citizen

Vice Presidents Nominated For President Of The United States Who Lost A Presidential Election

Al Gore	1993-2001	2000
George Bush	1981-1989	1992
Walter Mondale	1977-1981	1984
Gerald Ford	1973-1974	1976
Hubert Humphrey	1965-1969	1968
Richard Nixon	1953-1961	1960
Theodore Roosevelt	1901	1912
John Breckinridge	1857-1861	1860
John Adams	1789-1797	1800

Untimely Dismissals

Vice Presidents That Missed Being President Because They Died,
Were Replaced, or Resigned From Office

Hannibal Hamlin	1861–1865	1865	Abraham Lincoln and Hamlin had little interaction throughout the Civil War. Hamlin was replaced on Lincoln's Republican ticket with Democrat Andrew Johnson to help ensure victory. Johnson became Vice President and assumed the presidency upon the assassination of Lincoln.
Garret Hobart	1897–1899	Died in 1899	Upon Hobart's untimely death in 1899, Theodore Roosevelt was chosen to assume his spot as the vice presidential candidate in the 1900 election. The following summer, President William McKinley was assassinated and Roosevelt assumed the Presidency.
Henry Wallace	1941–1945	1945	Franklin Roosevelt dropped Wallace from the ticket in 1944 due to political pressure from his party, choosing Missouri Senator Harry Truman as his vice presidential running mate. Truman assumed the Presidency upon Roosevelt's death in 1945.
Spiro Agnew	1969–1973	1973	Agnew was elected to a second term, but when a scandal emerged about his past business practices, Agnew was forced to resign the Vice Presidency. President Richard Nixon selected Congressman Gerald Ford to replace him, and when Nixon was forced to resign in 1974, Ford became President.

VicePresidents.com

Poll Results

The Second Lady:	33%
Mrs. (Last Name):	27%
Mrs. Vice President:	21%
No Official Title or Designation:	19%

Resources

Although this work is comprised of facts and history, it should be noted that several books and websites have helped provide background and data. Those resources have been great assistance and are listed below.

Books

Anderson, Marilyn D. *The Vice Presidency.* 2001. Pennsylvania: Chelsea House Publishers.

Barzman, Sol. *Madmen and Geniuses, The Vice-Presidents of the United States.* 1974. Chicago, IL: Follett Publishing Company.

Dorman, Michael. *The Second Man, The Changing Role of the Vice Presidency.* 1968. New York: Delacorte Press.

Dunlap, Leslie W. *Our Vice-Presidents and Second Ladies.* 1988. The Scarecrow Press Inc.

Eskin, Blake. *The Book of Political Lists.* 1998. New York: Villard Books.

Feerick, John D. *The Twenty-Fifth Amendment, It's Complete History and Earliest Applications.* 1976. Fordham University.

Goldstein, Joel K. *The Modern American Vice Presidency, The Transformation of a Political Institution.* 1982. Princeton University Press.

Guerrero, Linda Dudik. *John Adams' Vice-Presidency.* 1982. New York: Arno Press.

Healy, Diana Dixon. *America's Vice Presidents: Our first forty-three VP's And How They Got To Be Number Two.* 1984. New York: Atheneum.

Hoopes, Roy. *The Changing Vice Presidency.* 1981. New York: Thomas Y. Crowell.

Kane, Joseph Nathan. *Presidential Fact Book.* 1999. Random House.

Kincade, Vance, Jr. *Heirs Apparent: Solving the Vice-Presidential Dilemma.* 2000. West Port, CT: Praeger Publishers.

Kuttner, Paul. *History's Trickiest Questions.* 1992. New York: Henry Holt and Company.

Light, Paul C. *Vice Presidential Power. Advice and Influence in the White House.* 1984. The Johns Hopkins University Press.

Purcell, L. Edward. *Vice Presidents, A Biographical Dictionary.* 2001. New York: Checkmark Books.

Feinberg, Barbara Silberdick. *Next in Line, The American Vice Presidency.* 1996. New York: Grolier Publishing.

Sindler, Allan. *Unchosen Presidents, The Vice President and Other Frustrations of Presidential Succession.* 1976. University of California Press, CA.

Southwick, Leslie H. *Presidential Also-Rans and Running Mates, 1788-1980.* 1984. McFarland & Company Inc.

Tally, Steve. *Bland Ambition. From Adams to Quayle.* 1992. Harcourt Brace Jovanovich, Publishers.

Vice Presidents of the United States and their Spouses. Courtesy of and with permission from David Hampton.

Walach, Timothy, Editor. *At The President's Side: The Vice Presidency in the Twentieth Century.* 1997. University of Missouri Press.

Young, Donald. *American Roulette. The History and Dilemma of the Vice Presidency.* 1965. Holt, Rinehart and Winston.

Websites

http://www.Senate.Gov.

http://politicalgraveyard.com

http://www.uselectionatlas.org.

http://www.nara.gov

http://www.WorldBook.com

http://www.cspan.org

http://www.unitedstates-on-line.com/vicepres.htm

http://www.usconstitution.net/constfaq.html

http://www.debates.org

http://www.alabamastuff.com

http://www.skyetech.net/politics/vp.html

http://www.washingtonpost.com

http://www.lycos.com

http://www.shabbir.com/nonmatchbox/usvpres.html

http://www.grolier.com

http://bioguide.congress.gov/scripts/biodisplay.pl?index=A000039

http://www.vpcentre.net

http://educate.si.edu/spotlight/july4.html

http://USATrivia.com

Learn More About The Vice Presidency And Its Vice Presidents

Check out

VicePresidents.com

at
www.VicePresidents.com

★ The only web magazine in the world that studies the Vice Presidency and its Vice Presidents.

★ Packed with facts, lists, trivia, links and more.

★ The best resource on the Vice Presidency and its Vice Presidents.

Collectors Edition Poster

"You *must have* this poster — it's amazing..."

"Only VicePresidents.com could have made this..."

"Light-hearted and colorful!"

Enjoy this one of a kind poster. Depicting all the Vice Presidents. A special poster that every fan of American politics should have.

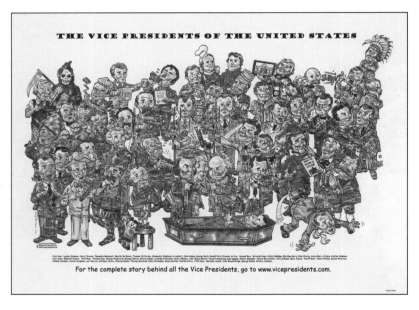

Order Today!

★ www.VicePresidents.com

★ www.eBay.com

★ 888-835-5326

★ VicePresidents1@yahoo.com

176

Order More Copies
Of This Book

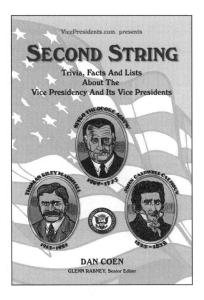

Five easy ways to order additional copies of this and other books from VicePresidents.com:

Order Today!

★ www.VicePresidents.com

★ www.Amazon.com

★ www.eBay.com

★ 888-835-5326

★ VicePresidents1@yahoo.com

Second String's First Team

Dan Coen, author, is managing director of VicePresidents.com, the world's leading on-line magazine dedicated to America's Vice Presidency and its Vice Presidents. In addition to books, VicePresidents.com features collector edition posters, links, news updates, historical analysis, biographies, facts and figures, trivia and interactive forums about the Vice Presidency and its Vice Presidents.

Glenn Rabney, Glenn Rabney, senior editor, has been a writer and editor for nearly 20 years and has been responsible for writing or producing more than 100 hours of television for HBO, PBS, Disney Channel, Family Channel and other outlets. He has been nominated for writing awards for his work on HBO's "Not Necessarily the News." He currently writes screenplays and resides in Tarzana, California with his wife and two daughters.

Jorge Pacheco, cartoonist, has been a working artist for 17 years, creating material for Dark House Comics, DC Comics, Harvey Comics, Archie Comics, Hanna Barbera, Warner Brothers. He has also provided art for Cracked Magazine, Jim Davis's Garfield, and numerous children's books. He lives and works in Santa Monica, California.